POLITICAL SCIENCE BIBLIOGRAPHIES

Volume I

by

Robert B. Harmon

California State University, San Jose

The Scarecrow Press, Inc.
Metuchen, N.J.   1973

Library of Congress Cataloging in Publication Data

Harmon, Robert Bartlett, 1932-
  Political science bibliographies.

  1. Bibliography--Bibliography--Political science.
I. Title.
Z7161.A1H35   016.01632   72-8849
ISBN 0-8108-0558-8

Copyright 1973 by Robert B. Harmon

To my Father and Mother-in-Law:

Marriner and Della Swensen

> "There are only two main theories of government in the world. One rests on righteousness and the other on force. One appeals to reason and the other appeals to the sword. One is exemplified in the republic, the other is represented by a despotism."
>
> Joseph Fielding Smith

CONTENTS

	Page
Preface	vii
Introduction	ix
Subject Bibliography	1
Author Index	141
Title Index	158

PREFACE

This volume is the first in a series which will attempt to list as many bibliographies published in the field of political science, or closely related areas, as possible. It is the culmination of two previous publications, A Bibliography of Bibliographies in Political Science (1964) and Sources and Problems of Political Science (1966). The format and organization have been redesigned to facilitate the retrieval of bibliographic information.

Bibliographies in the field of political science, as in the literature itself, are becoming more numerous. Consequently there is a need to maintain an accurate record for scholarly and informational use. The study of the orderly presentation of records has never been more necessary or difficult. Those seeking information in the field will need to master the techniques and uses of bibliography to further their understanding of our political world.

As in the case with my other works, the compiler is indebted to many who have contributed their time and efforts toward the completion of this project. Particularly to my wife is given thanks for her efforts in typing and editing the completed manuscript.

RBH

INTRODUCTION

A bibliography, indicates Verner W. Clapp, is a systematic listing, addressed to a particular purpose, of books and other materials which share common characteristics. There are many types of bibliographies, and bibliographers are not always in agreement with respect to defining the differences between them. Generally speaking, however, most of the bibliographic production related to the field of political science is systematic in nature and obviously subject oriented.

Items included in this bibliography are limited in several ways. First of all they are separately published bibliographies. Books containing bibliographies have not been included. Bibliographic articles appearing in journals have also been excluded. Wherever possible, brief annotations are provided, particularly with regard to additional subject areas contained within a bibliography.

The arrangement of entries has been devised to provide the user with a triangular approach to the retrieval of information. The body of the bibliography is arranged under subject headings which are as consistent as possible with those used by the Library of Congress. In addition separate author and title indexes are provided for further finding ease. Each item has a distinctive number affixed to it for identification. Where a bibliography has gone into more than one edition only the latest is included.

Below is a fictitious sample entry to illustrate the form and information included for each item:

^aPOLITICAL SOCIOLOGY

^b26.   ^cDoe, John James.   ^dA bibliography on political socialization.   ^eNew York, ^fDagmar Press, ^g1972.   ^h114p.   ⁱ(79-61134)

a. - Subject Heading
b. - Item number
c. - Author or Entry
d. - Title (underlined)
e. - Place of Publication
f. - Publisher
g. - Date of Publication
h. - Number of Pages
i. - Library of Congress Number

    Despite many problems associated with the compilation of bibliographies related to political science, the wealth of new ones and their constant improvement does make it possible for students and those engaged in research to approach their projects with increasing confidence. Greater coverage of the bibliographical universe of political science now makes it possible to be aware of what has been and is being done in various areas of the discipline.

SUBJECT BIBLIOGRAPHY

ADMINISTRATIVE LAW

1. Puget, Henry, ed. Essai de bibliographie des principaux ouvrages de droit public (droit public général, droit constitutionnel, droit administratif) de science politique et de science administrative qui ont paru hors de France de 1945 à 1958. Paris, Ed. de l'épargne, 1961. 369p. (NUC58-62)
    Includes along with administrative law items on constitutional law and political science.

AFRICA

2. African Bibliographic Center. The new Afro-Asian states in perspective, 1960-1963; a select bibliography. Washington, 1965. 20p. (66-50156)
    Includes items on the politics of the new states of Africa.

3. Gutkind, Peter Claus Wolfgang. A select bibliography on traditional and modern Africa. With John B. Webster. Syracuse, N.Y., Bibliographic Section, Program of Eastern African Studies, Syracuse University, 1968. 323 ℓ. (70-10279)

4. New Jersey. State College, Trenton. Roscoe L. West Library. Africa today; bibliography. Rev. ed. comp. by Parker Worley. Trenton, 1959. 23 ℓ. (60-62864)

Contains a number of items on African politics.

5. Venys, Ladislav. A select bibliography of Soviet publications on Africa in general and Eastern Africa in particular, 1962-1966. Syracuse, N.Y., Bibliographic Section, Program of Eastern African Studies, Syracuse University, 1968. 125 ℓ. (79-12531)
Contains items on Eastern Africa.

AFRICA--GOVERNMENT PUBLICATIONS

6. Boston University. Libraries. Catalog of African government documents and African area index. 2d ed., rev. and enl. Boston, G.K. Hall, 1964. 471p. (65-9838)
Covers also subject headings on Africa.

AFRICA--POLITICS

7. Alderfer, Harold Freed. A bibliography of African government, 1950-1966. 2d rev. ed. Lincoln University, Pa., Lincoln University Press, 1967. 163p. (67-27428)

AFRICA, EAST--POLITICS

8. Kasfir, Nelson. Bibliography on administration in East Africa. With Timothy M. Shaw. Kampala, Uganda, Dept. of Political Science and Public Administration, Makerere University College, 1968. 26 ℓ. (78-20973)

AFRICA, FRENCH WEST--GOVERNMENT PUBLICATIONS

9. U.S. Library of Congress. General Reference and Bibliography Division. Official publica-

tions of French West Africa, 1946-1958; a guide. Comp. by Helen F. Conover. Washington, 1960. 88p. (60-60036)

AFRICA, SOUTH--RACE QUESTION

10. United Nations. Secretariat. Apartheid; a selective bibliography on the racial policies of the Government of the Republic of South Africa. New York, 1970. 57p. (79-23584)
Also covers segregation in South Africa.

AFRICA, SUB-SAHARAN--POLITICS

11. Hertefelt, Marcel d'. African governmental systems in static and changing conditions. A bibliographic contribution to political anthropology. Tervuren, Musée royal de l'Afrique centrale, 1968. 178p. (74-474578)

AMERICAN BAR ASSOCIATION

12. American Bar Foundation. Cromwell Library. A check list of the special and standing committees of the American Bar Association. By Virgil L. Pederson ... Chicago, American Bar Foundation, 1964. 66p. (64-6928)

13. _____. A check list of publications of the sections and House of Delegates of the American Bar Association. Comp. by Edythe Keshner, bibliographer. Chicago, American Bar Foundation, 1961. 71p. (61-19966)

ANARCHISM AND ANARCHISTS

14. Nettlau, Max. Bibliographie de l'anarchie. Préf. d'Elisée Reclus. New York, B. Franklin, 1968. 294p. (68-56723)

ARAB COUNTRIES

15. Selim, George Dimitri. American doctoral dissertations on the Arab world, 1883-1968. Washington, Library of Congress, 1970. 103p. (79-607590)

ARISTOTELES

16. Schwab, Moïse. Bibliographie d'Aristote. New York, B. Franklin, 1967. 380p. (68-56729)

ARMED FORCES

17. Riddleberger, Peter B. A Preliminary bibliography on studies of the roles of military establishments in developing nations. Washington, Special Operations Research Office, American University, 1963. 1v. (67-65876)

ASIA

18. Kyriak, Theodore E. Asian developments: a bibliography. no. 1- Annapolis, Research Microfilms, 1962- . v. (62-20264)

19. New Jersey. State College, Trenton. Roscoe L. West Library. Asia today, a bibliography. Comp. by Parker Worley. Rev. ed. Trenton, 1960. 35 ℓ. (60-63181)

20. Yunesuko Higashi Ajia Bunka Kenkyū Sentā, Tokyo. A survey of bibliographies in Western languages concerning East and Southeast Asian studies. Tokyo, Centre for East Asian Cultural Studies, c1966. 227p. (70-5952)

ASIA, SOUTHEASTERN

21. Cordier, Henri. Bibliotheca Indosinica. Dic-

tionnaire bibliographique des ouvrages relatifs à la péninsule indochinoise. New York, B. Franklin, 1967. 5 v. in 3. (66-20681)

22. Harvard University. Library. <u>Southern Asia: Afghanistan, Bhutan, Burma, Cambodia, Ceylon, India, Laos, Malaya, Nepal, Pakistan, Sikkim, Singapore, Thailand, Vietnam.</u> Cambridge, Distributed by Harvard University Press, 1968. 543p. (68-15927)

23. Horne, Norman P. <u>A guide to published United States Government documents pertaining to Southeast Asia, 1893-1941.</u> Washington, 1961. 147 ℓ. (62-146)

24. Lian-The. <u>Treasures and trivia; doctoral dissertations on Southeast Asia accepted by universities in the United States.</u> Comp. with Paul W. van der Vevi. Athens, Ohio, Ohio University, Center for International Studies, 1968. 141p. (68-66324)
   Lists U.S. Doctoral dissertations on Southeast Asia.

25. <u>Southeast Asia: a bibliography for undergraduate libraries.</u> By Donald Clay Johnson and others. Williamsport, Pa., Bro-Dart Pub. Co., 1970. 59p. (73-122457)

AUSTRALIA--GOVERNMENT PUBLICATIONS

26. Finlayson, Jennifer Ann S. <u>Historical statistics of Australia; a select list of official sources.</u> Canberra, Dept. of Economic History, Research School of Social Sciences, Australian National University, 1970. 55p. (77-142737)

AUSTRALIA--POLITICS AND GOVERNMENT

27. Holmes, Joan (Craig), comp. <u>Bibliography of</u>

public administration in Australia, 1850-1947. Sydney, Dept. of Government and Public Administration, University of Sydney, 1956. 183p. (NUC53-7)

BAIL--U. S.

28. Tompkins, Dorothy Louise (Campbell) Culver. Bail in the United States: a bibliography. Berkeley, Institute of Governmental Studies, University of California, 1964. 49p. (64-65220)

BALKAN PENINSULA

29. Horecky, Paul Louis. Southeastern Europe: a guide to basic publications. Chicago, University of Chicago Press, 1969. 755p. (73-110336)

BALTIMORE METROPOLITAN AREA

30. Maryland. Morgan State College, Baltimore. Urban Studies Institute. Baltimore metropolitan area urban affairs bibliography. Baltimore, 1967. 70 ℓ. (77-630669)

BENTHAM, JEREMY, 1748-1832

31. London. University. University College. Library. Catalogue of the manuscripts of Jeremy Bentham in the Library of University College, London. Comp. by A. T. Milne. 2d ed. London, University of London, Athlone Press, 1962. 104p. (62-6679)

BERLIN QUESTION (1945-)

32. Deutsches Institut für Zeitgeschichte. Bibliothek. Deutsche Dissertationen zur Zeitgeschichte.

Auswahlbibliographie. Berlin, Deutsches Institut f. Zeitgeschichte, 1967. 211 ℓ. (72-509845) Also covers the history of the Federal Republic of Germany and the Democratic Republic of Germany.

BIBLIOGRAPHY

33. Besterman, Theodore. A world bibliography of bibliographies and of bibliographical catalogues, calendars, abstracts, digests, indexes, and the like. 4th ed., rev. and greatly enl. throughout. Lausanne, Societas Bibliographica, 1965-66. 5 v. (78-205303)

34. The Bibliographic index; a cumulative bibliography of bibliographies. v.1- . New York, H.W. Wilson, 1938- . v. (38-16461)

BIBLIOGRAPHY--BIBLIOGRAPHY--AFRICA

35. Garling, Anthea. Bibliography of African bibliographies. Cambridge, African Studies Centre, 1968. 1v. (76-362046)

BIBLIOGRAPHY--BIBLIOGRAPHY--GOVERNMENT PUBLICATIONS

36. International Committee for Social Sciences Documentation. Étude des bibliographies courantes des publications officielles nationales; guide sommaire et inventaire. Ed.: J. Meyriat. Paris, UNESCO, 1958. 260p. (58-425)

BIBLIOGRAPHY--BIBLIOGRAPHY--INTERNATIONAL RELATIONS

37. Boehm, Eric H., ed. Bibliographies on international relations and world affairs; an annotated

directory. Santa Barbara, Calif., Clio Press, 1965. 33p. (65-25555)
Also includes material on world politics, international law and area studies.

BIBLIOGRAPHY--BIBLIOGRAPHY--LATIN AMERICA

38. Gropp, Arthur Eric. A bibliography of Latin American bibliographies. Metuchen, N.J., Scarecrow Press, 1968. 515p. (68-9330)

BIBLIOGRAPHY--BIBLIOGRAPHY--LAW

39. U.S. Library of Congress. Law Library. Anglo-American legal bibliographies, an annotated guide. By W.L. Friend. Washington, U.S. Govt. Print. Off., 1944. 166p. (44-41314)
Contains bibliographies on U.S. and British law.

40. _____. The bibliography of international law and continental law. By E.M. Borchad. Washington, U.S. Govt. Print. Off., 1913. 93p. (12-35015)
Also covers international law and relations.

BIBLIOGRAPHY--BIBLIOGRAPHY--PERIODICALS

41. Gray, Richard A. Serial bibliographies in the humanities and social sciences. With D. Villmow. Ann Arbor, Mich., Pierian Press, 1969. 345p. (68-58895)
An extensive listing of periodicals carrying bibliographies.

BIBLIOGRAPHY--BIBLIOGRAPHY--SOCIAL SCIENCES

42. Otto, Frieda. Bibliographie wirtschafts- und sozialwissen-schaftlicher Bibliographien.

Zugänge der Bibliothek des Instituts für Weltwirtschaft, Kiel, in den Jahren 1962 bis 1967. Kiel, Institut für Weltwirtschaft, Bibliothek, 1968. 592p. (72-415363) Also covers economics.

BRAZIL--GOVERNMENT PUBLICATIONS

43. Mesa, Rosa Quintero. Brazil. Ann Arbor, Mich., University Microfilms, 1968. 343, 12p. (68-57259)

BRAZIL--POLITICS AND GOVERNMENT

44. Heimer, Franz-Wilhelm. Neuere Studien zur Politik Brasiliens, 1960-1967. With Maria de Lourdes Heimer and Mara Jorge Ramos. Freiburg i. Br., Arnold-Bergstraesser-Institut für Kulturwissenschaftliche Forschung, 1968. 91p. (76-400564)

BRIEFS--U.S.

45. Kenyon, Carleton W. Preparation of briefs; a bibliography. Sacramento, 1969. 7p. (NUC 69-140817)

BUKHARIN, NIKOLAI IVANOVICH, 1888-1938

46. Heitman, Sidney. Nikolai I. Bukharin; a bibliography, with annotations, incl. the locations of his works in major American and European libraries. Stanford, Hoover Institution on War, Revolution and Peace, Stanford University, 1969. 181p. (68-28101)

BULGARIA

47. Pundeff, Marin V. Bulgaria; a bibliographic guide. Washington, Slavic and Central European Division, Reference Department, Library of Congress, 1965. 98p. (65-60006)

BURKE, EDMUND, 1729?-1797

48. Todd, William Burton. A bibliography of Edmund Burke. London, Hart-Davis, 1964. 312p. (65-3904)

CALIFORNIA, LEGISLATURE

49. California. Legislature. Assembly. Legislative Reference Service. Bibliography of the California Legislature. Sacramento, 1965. 19 ℓ. (65-64602)

CALIFORNIA--POLITICS AND GOVERNMENT

50. Leister, D. R. California politics and problems, 1964-1968; a selective bibliography. Berkeley, Institute of Governmental Studies, University of California, 1969. 33 ℓ. (70-628573)

51. Leuthold, David A. California politics and problems, 1900-1963; a selective bibliography. With W. M. Reid and W. Macauley. Berkeley; Institute of Governmental Studies, University of California, 1965. 64p. (65-65223)

CANADA--GOVERNMENT PUBLICATIONS (PROVINCIAL GOVERNMENTS)

52. Bhatia, Mohan. Bibliographies, catalogues, checklists and indexes of Canadian provincial government publications. Saskatoon, University of Saskatchewan, Library, 1970. 16 ℓ. (74-558243)

CHINA

53. Cordier, Henri. Bibliotheca Sinica. Dictionnaire bibliographique des ouvrages relatifs à l'Empire chinois. 2. éd. rev., corr., et considérablement augm. New York, B. Franklin, 1968. v. in (68-58196)
    Also includes Chinese literature and classification of books.

54. Fairbank, John King. Japanese studies of modern China; a bibliographical guide to historical and social-science research on the 19th and 20th centuries. With Masataka Banno and Sumiko Yamamoto. Cambridge, Harvard University Press, 1971, c1955. 331p. (74-134948)

55. Gardner, Charles Sidney, comp. A union list of selected western books on China in American libraries. 2d ed. rev. and enl. New York, B. Franklin, 1970. 111p. (70-126971)
    Also includes libraries in Canada.

56. Hucker, Charles O. China; a critical bibliography. Tucson, University of Arizona Press, 1962. 125p. (62-10624)

57. Kyriak, Theodore E. China, 1957-July 1960; bibliography of United States Joint Publications Research Service translations on microfilm. Annapolis, Research & Microfilm Publications, 196-. 59p. (62-20268)

58. Mickey, Margaret Portia. A bibliography of South and Southwest China. Ann Arbor, University Microfilms, 1961? 161p. (NUC58-62)

59. Mote, Frederick W. Japanese-sponsored governments in China, 1937-1945; an annotated bibliography comp. from materials in the Chinese collection of the Hoover Library. Stanford, Stanford University Press, 1954. 68p. (55-854)

China--Biography

60. Uchida, Naosaku. The overseas Chinese; a bibliographical essay based on the resources of the Hoover Institution. With a suppl. bibliography by E. Wu, and Chün-tu Hsüeh. Stanford University, Calif., Hoover Institution on War, Revolution and Peace, Stanford University, 1959. 134p. (60-1670)

CHINA-BIOGRAPHY

61. Wu, Wên-chin. Leaders of twentieth-century China; an annotated bibliography of selected Chinese biographical works in the Hoover Library. Stanford, Calif., Stanford University Press, 1956. 106p. (56-13811)

CHINA--FOREIGN RELATIONS--GT. BRIT.

62. Gt. Brit. Foreign Office. Foreign Office confidential papers relating to China and her neighbouring countries, 1840-1914; with an Additional list 1915-1937. Comp. by Lo Hui-Min. The Hague, Paris, Mouton, 1969. 280p. (73-487894)
    Good coverage for the period 1840-1914.
    Also covers the Eastern question (Far East).

CHINA (PEOPLE'S REPUBLIC OF CHINA, 1949-   )

63. Harvard University. East Asian Research Center. Studies in social and political behavior and change: Communist China; final report. Cambridge, Mass., 1968. 11 ℓ. (NUC69-132672)

64. Kyriak, Theodore E. China: a bibliography. no. 1-3- Annapolis, Research Microfilms, 1962-   . v. (62-20262)

65. U.S. Dept. of the Army. Communist China: ruthless enemy or paper tiger? New York, Greenwood Press, 1969. 137p. (74-90730)

CHINA--POLITICS AND GOVERNMENT

66. Jiang, Joseph. Chinese bureaucracy and government administration, an annotated bibliography. Honolulu, Research Translations, East-West Center, 1964. 157 ℓ. (72-215194)

CITIES AND TOWNS--LATIN AMERICA

67. Sable, Martin Howard. Latin American urbanization; a guide to the literature, organizations, and personnel. Metuchen, N.J., Scarecrow Press, 1971. 1077p. (74-145643)

CITIES AND TOWNS--PLANNING

68. Branch, Melville Campbell. Comprehensive urban planning; a selective annotated bibliography with related materials. Beverly Hills, Calif., Sage Publications, 1970. 477p. (73-92349)

69. Duke, Richard D. Bibliography for gaming in urban research. East Lansing, Institute for Community Development and Services, Michigan State University, 1963. 4 ℓ. (64-64640)
    Also covers game theory, management games and decision-making.

70. Fritschler, A. Lee. Urban affairs bibliography; a guide to the literature in the field. Washington, School of Government and Public Administration, American University, 1970. 94p. (78-19138)
    Also includes Metropolitan government.

71. Guttenberg, Albert Z. Environmental reform in the United States: the Populist-Progressive era and the New Deal. Monticello, Ill., Council of Planning Librarians, 1969. 15 ℓ. (70-21593)
    Also includes regional planning.

72. Harrison, James D. An annotated bibliography on environmental perception with emphasis on urban areas. Monticello, Ill., Council of Planning Librarians, 1969. 41 ℓ. (75-23709)
    Also includes Human ecology and Urban sociology.

73. Lorenz, Robert. A world of cities; a cross-cultural urban bibliography. Syracuse, Center for Overseas Operations and Research, Maxwell Graduate School of Citizenship and Public Affairs, Syracuse University, 1964. 150p. (65-9006)
    Also includes urban sociology.

74. U.S. Air Force Academy. Library. The States and the urban crisis. Colorado Springs, 1969. 46p. (73-605758)

75. U.S. Dept. of Housing and Urban Development. New communities; a bibliography. Washington; U.S. Govt. Print. Off., 1970. 84p. (75-606174)

CIVIL DEFENSE

76. Malwad, N.M. Civil defence: an annotated bibliography, 1960-1968. Trombay, India, Bibliography Unit, Library & Technical Information Section, Bhabha Atomic Research Centre, 1970. 244p. (70-17277)

CIVIL LAW

77. Bibliographie des traductions des codes de droit privé des états membres du Conseil de l'Europe et de la Conférence de La Haye de droit international privé. Strasbourg, Conseil de l'Europe, 1967. 355p. (76-534906)

CIVIL RIGHTS--U.S.

78. Brooks, Alexander D. <u>Civil rights and liberties in the United States, an annotated bibliography.</u> With a selected list of fiction and audio-visual materials. With V. H. Ellison. New York, Civil Liberties Educational Foundation, c1962. 151p. (62-51084)
Also covers race problems.

CIVIL SERVICE

79. Greer, Sarah. <u>A bibliography of civil service and personnel administration.</u> New York, and London, McGraw-Hill, 1935. 143p. (35-1947)
Also covers employment management and employment of women.

CIVIL SERVICE POSITIONS--U.S.

80. U.S. Civil Service Commission. <u>Guide to Federal career literature.</u> Washington, U.S. Govt. Print. Off., 1969. 32p. (70-604114)

CIVIL SERVICE POSITIONS--U.S.--CLASSIFICATION.

81. U.S. Civil Service Commission. <u>Position classification and pay in the Federal Government.</u> Washington, 1970. 63p. (78-608832)
Also covers U.S. officials' and employees' salaries and allowances.

CIVILIZATION

82. American Universities Field Staff. <u>A select bibliography: Asia, Africa, Eastern Europe, Latin America.</u> New York, 1960. 534p.

College Students 16

_____. _____. Supplement, 1961- .
New York. v. (60-10482rev.)

COLLEGE STUDENTS--POLITICAL ACTIVITY

83. Altbach, Philip G. Student politics and higher education in the United States; a select bibliography. With R. Graham. Introd. essay by S. M. Lipset. Rev. ed. St. Louis, United Ministries in Higher Education, 1968. 86p. (68-54908)
   Deals exclusively with the political activity of college students.

COLOMBIA--GOVERNMENT PUBLICATIONS

84. Mesa, Rosa Quintero. Colombia. Ann Arbor, Mich., University Microfilms, 1968. 137, 3p. (68-56197)

COLOMBIA--POLITICS AND GOVERNMENT

85. Ziervogel, Barbara. Kolumbien. Neuere Studien 1958-1969. Bielefeld, Bertelsmann-Universitätsverl., 1969. 85p. (77-506019)
   Also covers economic conditions, social conditions and history of Colombia.

COLONIES

86. Collotti Pischel, Enrica. L'Internationale communiste et les problèmes coloniaux, 1919-1935. With C. Robertazzi. Paris, La Haye, Mouton & Co., 1968. 584p. (70-413418)
   Also covers imperialism.

COLORADO--POLITICS AND GOVERNMENT

87. Colorado. University. Bureau of Governmental Research and Service. A selected bibliography of Colorado State and local government. By Morris J. Schur, research assistant. Boulder, 1964. 99p. (64-64433)

COMMERCIAL CRIMES--U. S.

88. Tompkins, Dorothy Louise (Campbell) Culver. White collar crime; a bibliography. Berkeley, Institute of Governmental Studies, University of California, 1967. 85p. (67-64649)

COMMERCIAL LAW--U. S.

89. Marke, Julius J. Commercial law: information sources. With E.J. Bander. Detroit, Gale Research Co., 1970. 220p. (73-120909)

COMMONWEALTH OF NATIONS

90. National Book League, London. Readers guide to the Commonwealth. London, National Book League, 1970. 210p. (72-540340)

COMMUNISM

91. Dutschke, Rudi. Ausgewählte und kommentierte Bibliographie des revolutionären Sozialismus von K. Marx bis in die Gegenwart. Heidelberg, Druck-und Verlagskooperative, 1969. 49p. (77-537805)

92. Hunt, Robert Nigel Carew. Books on communism, a bibliography. London, Ampersand Ltd., 1959. 333p. (60-234)

93. Kyriak, Theodore E. International communist development, 1957-1961; an index and guide to a

collection of US JPRS translations emanating from Africa, Latin America and Western Europe. Annapolis, Research Microfilms, 1962. 54 ℓ. (62-20270)

94. _____. International Communist development, 1962 (January-June). Annapolis, Research & Microfilm Publications, 196-. 32p. (66-1109)

95. Ruffmann, Karl Heinz. Kommunismus in Geschichte und Gegenwart. Mit Werner John. 2., wesentl. erw. Aufl. Bonn, Bundeszentrale f. Politische Bildung, 1966. 453p. (78-239531) Also covers Communist countries.

COMMUNISM--CHINA

96. Cole, Allan Burnett. Fifty years of Chinese communism: selected readings with commentary. With Peter C. Oleson. 2d ed. Washington, Service Center for Teachers of History, 1969. 50p. (75-108422)

COMMUNISM--HUNGARY

97. Gáliczky, Éva. Történelem, forradalom; a magyar munkászmozgalom történetéről megjelent legujabb könyvek ajánló bibliográfiája. Budapest, Fővárosi Szabó Ervin Könyvtár, 1966. 63p. (71-243604)
Also covers labor and laboring classes of Hungary.

COMMUNISM--SPANISH AMERICA

98. California. University. University at Los Angeles. Center of Latin American Studies. Communism in Latin America, a bibliography; the post-war years (1945-1960). Comp. by Ludwig Lauerhass, Jr. Los Angeles, 1962. 78p. (62-63357)

COMMUNISM--U. S.

99. Bibliography on the Communist problem in the United States. New York City, Fund for the Republic, 1955. 474p. (55-2164)

100. Delaney, Robert Finley. The literature of communism in America; a selected reference guide. Washington, Catholic University of America Press, 1962. 433p. (62-6923)

101. Seidman, Joel Isaac. Communism in the United States; a bibliography. With Olive Golden and Yaffa Draznin. Ithaca, N.Y., Cornell University Press, 1969. 526p. (69-12427)
General and extensive coverage.

COMMUNITY DEVELOPMENT

102. Argentine Republic. Congreso. Biblioteca. Referencia General. Desarrollo de la comunidad. Buenos Aires, 1967. 8 ℓ. (78-245230)
Also covers social change.

103. Shiner, Patricia. Community development in urban areas; a summary of pertinent journal articles and book chapters. With P. Wireman and L.J. Cary. Columbia, Dept. of Regional and Community Affairs, University of Missouri, 1969. 81p. (76-627934)

104. Singapore (City). National Library. Urban community development, Singapore, 1962. 26p. (70-237334)

COMMUNITY DEVELOPMENT--PAKISTAN

105. Azim, M. A bibliography of Academy publications, 1959-69. Peshawar, Pakistan Academy for Rural Development, 1970. 48p. (72-931767)

COMPARATIVE GOVERNMENT

106. U.S. Library of Congress. Division of Bibliography. A selected list of recent books on modern political systems. Comp. by Grace Hadley Fuller. Washington, 1936. 26p.

COMPARATIVE LAW

107. Szladits, Charles. A bibliography on foreign and comparative law; books and articles in English. New York, Parker School of Foreign and Comparative Law, Columbia University; 1955. 508p. (55-11076)
    Also includes conflict of laws.

CONSERVATION OF NATURAL RESOURCES

108. National Book League, London. Man and environment. London, National Book League in association with the Nature Conservancy, 1970. 31p. (75-484366)
    Also includes man's influence on nature.

109. Paulsen, David F. Natural resources in the governmental process; a bibliography selected and annotated. Tucson, University of Arizona Press, 1970. 99p. (77-121895)

CONSTITUTIONAL CONVENTIONS--NEW YORK (STATE)

110. New York (State). State Library. Albany. Legislative Reference Library. Constitutional revision in the Empire State: a bibliography. Albany, 1967. 8p. (75-629944)
    Also covers Constitutional history of New York state.

Constitutions

CONSTITUTIONS, STATE--U. S.--AMENDMENTS

111. Halévy, Balfour J. A selective bibliography on State constitutional revision. With L. H. Guth. New York, National Municipal League, 1963. 177 ℓ. (64-57206)

112. National Municipal League. State constitutions and constitutional revision; a selected bibliography. New York, 1962. 16 ℓ. (NUC65-33706)
Also covers legal bibliography.

COUNTY GOVERNMENT--TENNESSEE--RECORDS AND CORRESPONDENCE--INDEXES

113. Tennessee. State Library and Archives, Nashville. Archives Section. Inventories of Tennessee county records on microfilm. Nashville, 19-? v. (79-17432)
Also covers Tennessee Archives and documents on microfilm.

COURT OF JUSTICE OF THE EUROPEAN COMMUNITIES

114. Court of Justice of the European Communities. Bibliographie zur europäischen Rechtsprechung betreffend die Entscheidung zu den Verträgen über die Gründung der Europäischen Gemeinschaften. Bibliographie de jurisprudence européenne ... n. p., Cour de justice des communautés européennes, 1965. 261p. (77-515450)
Also includes Law in European Economic Community countries.

CRIME AND CRIMINALS

115. Cumming, Sir John Ghest. A contribution towards

a bibliography dealing with crime and cognate subjects. 3d ed. Montclair, N.J., Patterson Smith, 1970. 107p. (71-108220)
Also includes Criminal law.

116. Social Science Research Council. Committee on Survey of Research on Crime and Criminal Justice. A guide to material on crime and criminal justice. Montclair, N.J., Patterson Smith, 1969, c1929. 665p. (69-16240)
Also covers criminal justice and its administration and criminal law in the United States.

117. Vandiver, Richard. A selected bibliography of paperback books on crime. With J. Lewis. Carbondale, Center for the Study of Crime, Delinquency and Corrections, Southern Illinois University, 1970. 33p. (76-631937)

CRIMINAL JUSTICE, ADMINISTRATION OF--U.S.

118. California. University. Institute of Governmental Studies. Administration of criminal justice, 1949-1956; a selected bibliography. Comp. by D.C. Tompkins. Montclair, N.J., Patterson Smith, 1970. 351p. (77-108219)

119. ———. Bibliography of crime and criminal justice, 1927-1931. Comp. by D.C. Culver. Montclair, N.J., Patterson Smith, 1969. 413p. (69-16228)

120. ———. Bibliography of Crime and criminal justice, 1932-1937. Comp. by D.C. Culver. Montclair, N.J., Patterson Smith, 1969. 391p. (69-16227)

121. ———. Sources for the study of the administration of criminal justice, 1938-1949; a selected bibliography. Comp. by D.C. Tomp-

kins. Montclair, N.J., Patterson Smith, 1970. 294p. (73-108218)

CRIMINAL LAW

122. Böhmer, Georg Wilhelm. Handbuch der Litteratur des Criminalrechts. In seinen allgemeinen Beziehungen, mit besondrer Rücksicht auf Criminalpolitik nebst wissenschaftlichen Bemerkungen. Amsterdam, Rodopi, 1970. 888p. (70-510148)

CRIMINAL PROCEDURE--U.S.

123. Tompkins, Dorothy Louise (Campbell) Culver. The confession issue from McNabb to Miranda: a bibliography. Berkeley, Institute of Governmental Studies, University of California, 1968. 100p. (68-64269)

CUBA

124. Revolutionary Cuba; a bibliographical guide. v. Coral Gables, Fla., University of Miami Press, 1966- . (68-21369)

CZECHOSLOVAK REPUBLIC

125. Engová, Helena. Bibliografie k dějinám ČSR a KSČ 1917-1938. Historiografická produkee za léta 1945-1967. With Miloš Měštánek and Květa Náhlovská. Praha, Knihovna Ustavu dějin socialismu, 1968. 4 v. (70-415865)
Also covers the history of the Czechoslovak Republic.

DECISION-MAKING

126. Wasserman, Paul. Decision-making; an anno-

tated bibliography. With Fred S. Silander. Ithaca, N.Y., Graduate School of Business and Public Administration, Cornell University, 1958. 111p. (58-4160 rev)

DENMARK--FOREIGN RELATIONS

127. Sørensen, Per. Fortegenelse over dansk materiale til studiet af skandinavisk forsvars-og alliancepolitik 1848-1950. Under tilsyn af Ole Karup Pedersen. København, Københavns universitets institut for samtidshistorie og statskundskale, 1965. 69 ℓ. (78-375789)
   Also includes Foreign relations of Norway, Sweden and Finland.

DIPLOMATIC PRIVILEGES AND IMMUNITIES

128. Essen, Jan Louis Frederk van. Immunities in international law. With J.L.G. Tichelaar. Leyden, A.W. Sijthoff, 1955. 56p. (57-90)

DISARMAMENT

129. Collart, Yves. Disarmament; a study guide and bibliography on the efforts of the United Nations. The Hague, M. Nijhoff, 1958. 110p. (59-768)

DISCRIMINATION IN EMPLOYMENT--U.S.

130. U.S. Federal Aviation Administration. Library Services Division. Equal employment opportunity; selected references. Comp. by D.J. Poehlman. Washington, 1968. 7p. (77-601035)
   Includes employment of Negroes.

DOMINICAN REPUBLIC--POLITICS AND GOVERNMENT

131. Wiarda, Howard J. Materials for the study of politics and government in the Dominican Republic, 1930-1966. Santiago de los Caballeros, UCMM, 1968. 142p. (71-22412)

EAST (FAR EAST)

132. Borg, Dorothy. The Far East, a bibliography. With Hugh Borton for the American Council of the Institute of Pacific Relations. (In the Booklist. Chicago, American Library Association, 1942. v. 38, no. 14, pt. 2, p. 289-294) (42-51168)

133. Bulletin of Far Eastern bibliography. Washington, D.C., Committees on Far Eastern Studies of the American Council of Learned Societies, 1936-1941. 5v. (42-6022)

134. Tsien, Tsuen-hsuin. East Asia: checklist of literature proposed for micro-publishing. Zug, Inter Documentation Company, 1967? 56p. (74-414195)

135. U.S. Dept. of State. External Research Division. East Asia. Washington, Oct. 1958- . no. (60-64639)

EASTERN QUESTION (FAR EAST)

136. Buell, Raymond Leslie. Problems of the Pacific, a brief bibliography. Prepared for the American Council of the Institute of Pacific Relations. Boston, World Peace Foundation, 1925. 34p. (25-14407)

ECONOMIC ASSISTANCE, BRITISH

137. Gt. Brit. Ministry of Overseas Development. Li-

brary. Select bibliography on British aid to developing countries. 2nd ed. London, Ministry of Overseas Development, 1969. 20p. (74-537038)

ECONOMIC DEVELOPMENT

138. Geiger, H. Kent. National development, 1776-1966; a selective and annotated guide to the most important articles in English. Metuchen, N.J., Scarecrow Press, 1969. 247p. (77-5813)
    Also covers social change and social history of the 20th century.

ELECTION DISTRICTS--U.S.--STATES

139. Silva, Ruth Caridad. Selected bibliography on legislative apportionment and districting. With W.J.D. Boyd. New York, National Municipal League, 1963. 51 ℓ. (NUC65-41082)
    Covers the election law concerning apportionment.

ELECTIONS

140. Goodey, Brian R. The geography of elections, an introductory bibliography. Grand Forks, Center for the Study of Cultural and Social Change, University of North Dakota, 1968? 64p. (73-632559)

ELECTIONS--U.S.--STATISTICS

141. Burnham, Walter Dean. Sources of historical election data, a preliminary bibliography. East Lansing, Institute for Community Development and Services, Michigan State University, 1963. 20p. (64-64644)

ELITE (SOCIAL SCIENCES)

142. Beck, Carl. Political elites; a select computerized bibliography. With J.T. McKechnie. Cambridge, Mass., M.I.T. Press, 1968. 661p. (67-27338)
    A bibliography of approximately 4,000 items from books, and periodicals containing information relevant to the study of political elites in all areas.

EMPLOYEE-MANAGEMENT RELATIONS IN GOVERNMENT

143. Pegnetter, Richard. Public employment bibliography. Ithaca, New York State School of Industrial and Labor Relations, Cornell University, 1971. 49p. (70-22417)

ENVIRONMENTAL POLICY--U.S.

144. Juris, Gail. From now on... an environmental bibliography. With M. Medling. St. Louis, 1970. 46p. (78-275932)
    Also covers ecology in the U.S.

145. Meshenberg, Michael J. Environmental planning: a selected annotated bibliography. Chicago, American Society of Planning Officials, c1970. 78p. (70-22732)

ETHIOPIA

146. Matthews, Daniel G. A current bibliography on Ethiopian affairs; a select bibliography from 1950-1964. Washington, African Bibliographic Center, 1965. 46p. (66-50165)

EUROPE, EASTERN

147. Horecky, Paul Louis. East Central Europe; a guide to basic publications. Chicago, University of Chicago Press, 1969. 956p. (70-79472)

148. Kyriak, Theodore E. East Europe: a bibliography. no. 1-3-July-Sept. 1962- . Annapolis, Research Microfilms. v. (62-20261)

149. U.S. Dept. of the Army. Communist Eastern Europe; analytical survey of literature. Washington, U.S. Govt. Print. Off., 1971. 367p. (78-611513)
    Covers the politics of Eastern Europe.

EUROPE, EASTERN--LAW

150. Gumpert, Ute. Useful translations of East European statutes in French and German. Chicago, University of Chicago Law School, 1969. 43p. (NUC70-21229)

EUROPEAN ECONOMIC COMMUNITY

151. Macdonald, Hugh Ian. The European Economic Community: background & bibliography. Toronto, Canadian Institute of International Affairs, 1962. 16p. (63-3220)

152. Ortak Pazar bibliyoğrafyasi. Ankara, Türkiye Ticaret Odaloari, Sanayi Odalari ve Ticaret Borsalari Birliği Kütüphanesi. no. in v. 1969- . (73-268577)

153. Publications of the European Communities. Catalogue. Luxembourg, Publications Dept. of the European Communities. v. (76-22345)
    Also includes works on European Coal and

Steel Community and the European Atomic Energy Community.

154. Tamuno, Olufunmilayo G. The E.E.C. and developing nations, 1958-1966; a bibliography. Ibadan, Nigerian Institute of Social and Economic Research, 1967. v.1, 51p. (76-5601)
Also includes underdeveloped areas.

EUROPE--ECONOMIC INTEGRATION

155. California. State College, San Diego. Library. Bibliography on European integration; list of the books, documents, and periodicals on European integration in San Diego State College Library. Comp. by A. Szabo and W.H. Posner. San Diego, 1967. 62p. (68-64202)
Also includes works on European politics.

156. Cosgrove, Carol Ann. A readers' guide to Britain and the European communities. London, P.E.P., 1970. 106p. (75-535497)
Also covers the European Economic Community and Britain.

157. Hamburg, Europa-Kolleg. Auswahlbibliographie zur europäischen Integration. Hamburg. 1963. 87p. (70-235009)
Also includes works on Europe's politics.

158. Organization for European Economic Cooperation. Bibliographies de l'OECE. no. 1- . Paris, 1956- . (65-80948)
Also includes economics in general.

EUROPEAN FEDERATION

159. Medsker, Karen. European international organizations and integration movements: reports and analyses. A selected bibliography of non-book materials appearing between 1965 and early

1970. Bloomington, Bureau of Public Discussion, Indiana University, 1970. 7 ℓ. (74-631641)

160. Paklons, L. L. Bibliographie européenne. Bruges, De Tempel, 1964. 217p. (65-58174)

FEDERAL GOVERNMENT

161. Bachelder, Glen L. Federalism, a selected bibliography. With Paul C. Shaw. East Lansing, Institute for Community Development and Services, Michigan State University, 1964. 20p. (64-64645)

162. Liboiron, Albert A. Federalism and intergovernmental relations in Australia, Canada, the United States and other countries; a bibliography. Kingston, Ont., Institute of Intergovernmental Relations, Queen's University, 1967. 231 ℓ. (68-110060)

FEDERAL GOVERNMENT--U. S.

163. U. S. Commission on Intergovernmental Relations. Intergovernmental relations in the United States: a selected bibliography on interlevel and interjurisdictional relations. Prepared by W. B. Graves for the Commission... Washington, 1955. 207p. (55-61502)
  Also includes works on Grants-in-aid in the United States.

FIJI ISLANDS--GOVERNMENT PUBLICATIONS

164. Baksh, S. Serial publications of the Government of Fiji. Rev. and enl. by L. S. Qalo. Suva, Central Archives of Fiji and the Western Pacific High Commission, 1970. 16 ℓ. (79-21571)

Finland

FINLAND--GOVERNMENT PUBLICATIONS

165. Finland. Valtion painatuskeskus. Luettelo.
Helsinki. v.
. Lisäluettelo. Helsinki. v. (77-558722)

FRANCE--POLITICS AND GOVERNMENT

166. Heinz, Grete. The French Fifth Republic, establishment and consolidation (1958-1965); an annotated bibliography of the holdings at the Hoover Institution. With A. F. Peterson. Stanford, Calif., Hoover Institution Press, 1970. 170p. (70-92497)
Covers modern French government and politics.

167. Lindsay, Robert O. French political pamphlets, 1547-1648; a catalog of major collections in American libraries. With J. Neu. Madison, University of Wisconsin Press, 1969. 510p. (78-84953)
Covers French politics and government in the 16th and 17th centuries.

FRANKFURTER, FELIX, 1882-1965

168. U.S. Library of Congress. Manuscript Division. Felix Frankfurter: a register of his papers in the Library of Congress. Washington, Library of Congress, 1971. 70p. (76-609869)

GAME THEORY

169. U.S. Dept. of State. External Research Staff. Game theory and its application to the social sciences; a bibliography. Washington, 1964. 12p. (64-61256)

GEORGIA--POLITICS AND GOVERNMENT

170. Turnbull, Augustus B. Selected bibliography on Georgia government. With R. Spence. Athens, Institute of Government, University of Georgia, 1968. 96 ℓ. (76-626831)
    General coverage of Georgia politics and government

GERMANY--FOREIGN RELATIONS

171. Carlson, Andrew R. German foreign policy, 1890-1914, and colonial policy to 1914; a handbook and annotated bibliography. Metuchen, N.J., Scarecrow Press, 1970. 333p. (72-9539)
    Good general coverage of materials on German foreign relations between 1888-1914.

172. Jäger, Eckhard. Die deutsch-französischen Beziehungen im Spiegel der DDR-Literatur. Eine Bibliographie. Lüneburg (Ost-Akademie), 1968. 60p. (74-496058)
    Introductory material in German and French.

173. Riesser, Hans Eduard. Aussenpolitische Memoiren, Aufzeichnungen und Briefe deutscher Staatsoberhaüpter, Reichs-, Bundeskanzler, Aussenminister und Angehöriger des Auswärtigen Amtes. Eine Bibliographie als Beitrag zur Geschichte des Auswärtigen Amtes und der auswärtigen Politik von Bismarck bis Adenauer. 4. Fassung. Bonn, Bouvier in Kommission, 1966. 15p. (67-97170)

GERMANY--POLITICS AND GOVERNMENT

174. Faber, Karl Georg. Die nationalpolitische

Publizistik Deutschlands von 1866 bis 1871; eine kritische Bibliographie. Hrsg. von der Kommission für Geschichte des Parlamentarismus und der politischen Partein. Düsseldorf, Droste Verlag, 1963. 2 v. (65-71354)
Also covers German history between 1848-1870.

GERMANY (DEMOCRATIC REPUBLIC, 1949-   )

175. Berlin. Stadtbibliothek. Von der Wartburg bis nach Usedom: Bücher beraten Urlauber und Erholungssuchende. Eine Auswahlbibliographie. Berlin, 1959. 64p. Nachtrag 1959-1962. Berlin, 1962. 50p. (73-247014)

176. Leipzig. Stadt- und Bezirksbibliothek. Unser Staat, unser Stolz. (Auswahlbibliographie. Erarb. von einer Arbetisgruppe unter Leitg. von Christa Wolff und Gisela Piater.) Leipzig, 1969. 2 v. (79-531622)
    Also includes works on German literature.

GERMANY (DEMOCRATIC REPUBLIC, 1949-   )--FOREIGN RELATIONS--TREATIES

177. Bonn. Archiv für Gesamtdeutsche Fragen. Zusammenstellung der von der "Deutschen Demokratischen Republik" seit deren Gründung (7. Oktober 1949) abgeschlossenen internationalen Verträge und Vereinbarungen. Zasammengestellt von Lothar Kapsa. 5 Aufl. Stand: November 1967. Bonn, 1967. 232p. (76-562388)

GHANA

178. Adams, Cynthia. A study guide for Ghana; a bibliography. Boston, Boston University, African Studies Center, Development Program, 1967. 95p. (76-270973)

GHANA--GOVERNMENT PUBLICATIONS

179. Witherell, Julian W. Ghana; a guide to official publications, 1872-1968. With S.B. Lockwood. Washington, General Reference and Bibliography Division, Library of Congress, 1969. 110p. (74-601680)
    Covers most types of government publications issued in Ghana since 1872.

GOVERNMENT BUSINESS ENTERPRISES--INDIA

180. Indian Institute of Public Administration. A bibliography on public enterprises in India. New Delhi, 1968. 135p. (73-912768)

GOVERNMENT PUBLICATIONS

181. Alaska. State Library, Juneau. State publications received. 1965- . v. (66-64642)

182. United Nations. Dag Hammerskjold Library. Annotated list of official gazettes. Rev. draft ed. New York, 1962. 70 ℓ. (NUC65-24341)

183. Wilcox, Jerome Kear. Bibliography of new guides and aides to public documents use, 1953-1956. New York, Special Libraries Association, 1957. 16p. (57-9153)

GRANTS-IN-AID--U. S.

184. U. S. Library of Congress. Legislative Reference Service. Bibliography of Federal grants-in-aid to State and local governments, 1964-1969. Prep. for the Subcommittee on Intergovernmental Relations (pursuant to S. Res. 310, 91st Cong.) of the Committee on Government Operations, United States Senate. Washington, U. S. Govt. Print. Off., 1970. 456p. (76-610490)

GT. BRIT.--CONSTITUTIONAL HISTORY

185. Cam, Helen Maud. Bibliography of English constitutional history. With A. S. Turberville. London, G. Bell, 1929. 32p. (29-5925)

GT. BRIT.--GOVERNMENT PUBLICATIONS

186. Colchester, Eng. University of Essex. Library. British government publications. Colchester (Essex), University of Essex (Library), 1968. 7p. (70-530218)

187. Coolidge, John E. A brief guide to the use of the government documents of Great Britain and the United States. With R. S. McGregor and William R. Petrowski. Omaha, 1968. 14 ℓ. (76-14101)
Covers only the more basic items.

188. Gt. Brit. Central Office of Information. Reference Division. Catalogue of reference documents. London. v. (74-19693)
Also includes works on reference books.

189. Gt. Brit. Public Record Office. List of Cabinet papers 1915 and 1916. London, H. M. S. O., 1966. 112p. (66-73167)

Gt. Brit. 36

190. Gt. Brit. Stationery Office. <u>Government publications catalogue,</u> 1923- . v.

191. Pemberton, John E. <u>British official publications.</u> Oxford, New York, Pergamon Press, 1971. 315p. (77-137136)

GT. BRIT.--POLITICS AND GOVERNMENT

192. Royal Institute of Public Administration. <u>British Public administration: a select bibliography.</u> London, 1963. 22p. (NUC65-87756)

HAGUE. PERMANENT COURT OF INTERNATIONAL JUSTICE

193. Douma, J., comp. <u>Bibliography on the International Court including the Permanent Court, 1918-1964.</u> Leyden, A.W. Sijthoff, 1966, c1965. 387p.
Good coverage of the subject as well as international law.

194. Hague. International Court of Justice. <u>Publications of the International Court of Justice; catalogue.</u> Hague, 1957. 16p. (60-37707)

GT. BRIT. COLONIAL OFFICE

195. Gt. Brit. Public Record Office. <u>List of Colonial Office confidential print to 1916.</u> London, H.M. Stationery Off., 1965. 179p. (65-8691)

196. _____. <u>List of Colonial Office records, preserved in the Public Record Office.</u> New York, Kraus Reprint Corp., 1963. 337p. (66-34181)

GT. BRIT. FOREIGN OFFICE

197. Gt. Brit. Public Record Office. List of Foreign Office records. New York, Kraus Reprint Corp., 1964- . v. (65-3164)

198. ———. List of Foreign Office records to 1878 preserved in the Public Record Office. New York, Kraus Reprint Corp., 1963. 489p. (66-34180)

199. ———. The records of the Foreign Office 1782-1939. London, H. M. Stationery Off., 1969. 180p. (76-459641)

GT. BRIT. PARLIAMENT. HOUSE OF COMMONS. SESSIONAL PAPERS--INDEXES

200. Rodgers, Frank. Serial publications in the British Parliamentary papers, 1900-1968; a bibliography. Chicago, American Library Association, 1971. 146p. (74-117628)

HAND, LEARNED, 1872-1961.

201. Breuer, Ernest Henry. Learned Hand, January 27, 1872-August 18, 1961: bibliography. Albany, University of the State of New York, State Education Dept., New York State Library, 1964. 18p. (A65-7324)

HAWAII--GOVERNMENT PUBLICATIONS

202. Hawaii. Dept. of Planning and Economic Development. Hawaii State research inventory, 1961-1966. Honolulu, 1967. 199 ℓ. (74-632342)
    Covers Hawaiian government publications and research.

HAWAII--POLITICS AND GOVERNMENT

203. Terauchi, Mildred. Hawaiian politics, 1945-1961; a selected bibliography. With D. W. Tuttle, Jr. Honolulu, Program in Political Parties, Dept. of Govt., University of Hawaii, 1962. 7 ℓ. (64-63101)

HOBBES, THOMAS, 1588-1679

204. Macdonald, Hugh. Thomas Hobbes; a bibliography. With M. Hargreaves. London, Bibliographical Society, 1952. 83p. (A53-3337)

HOLMES, OLIVER WENDELL, 1809-1894

205. Currier, Thomas Franklin. A bibliography of Oliver Wendell Holmes. Ed. by E. M. Tilton for the Bibliographical Society of America. New York, Russell & Russell, 1971, c1953. 707p. (70-139916)

HOOKER, RICHARD, 1553 or 4-1600

206. Hill, William Speed. Richard Hooker, a descriptive bibliography of the early editions: 1593-1724. Cleveland, Press of Case Western Reserve University, 1970. 140p. (72-147090)

207. Woolley, Harry Clark. Thomas Hooker; bibliography, complete as known to date; together with a brief sketch of his life. Hartford, 1932. 32p. (71-240113)

HOUSING

208. U. S. Dept. of Housing and Urban Development. Library. Bibliography on housing, building, and planning, for use of overseas missions

of the United States Agency for International Development. Washington, 1969. 43p. (75-608633)
Also covers building.

HUNGARY--HISTORY--REVOLUTION, 1918-1919

209. Völgyes, Iván. The Hungarian Soviet Republic, 1919; an evaluation and a bibliography. Stanford, Calif., Hoover Institution Press, 1970. 90p. (70-108958)

HUNGARY--HISTORY--REVOLUTION, 1956-

210. Halasz de Beky, I. L. A bibliography of the Hungarian revolution, 1956. Toronto, University of Toronto Press, c1963. 179p. (64-4130)

INDIA--GOVERNMENT PUBLICATIONS

211. India (Republic). Government of India Publication Branch. List of official publications not included in the general catalogue government of India publications, issued during the period 1-1-1940 to 31-12-1960. Delhi, Manager of Publications, 1967. 95p. (76-909596)

INDIA--HISTORY--BRITISH OCCUPATION, 1765-1947

212. Aziz, Khursheed Kamal. The historical background of Pakistan, 1857-1947; an annotated digest of source material. Karachi, Pakistan Institute of International Affairs, 1970. 626p. (71-932004)
Also covers the Pakistan movement and Muslims in India.

213. Cohn, Bernard S. The development and impact

of British administration in India; a bibliographic essay. New Delhi, Indian Institute of Public Administration, 1961. 88p. (77-22033)

INDIANS OF NORTH AMERICA

214. Hargrett, Lester. A bibliography of the constitutions and laws of the American Indians. With an introd. by J. R. Swanton. Cambridge, Harvard Univ. Press, 1947. 124p. (47-31330)

215. U.S. Dept. of the Interior. Library. Biographical and historical index of American Indians and persons involved in Indian affairs. Boston, G.K. Hall, 1966. 8 v. (77-5470)

INDONESIA

216. Kyriak, Theodore E. Indonesia, 1957-1961; a bibliography and guide to contents of a collection of United States Joint Publications Research Service translations on microfilm. Annapolis, Research & Microfilm Publications, 196-. 34p. (62-20269)

INDONESIA--POLITICS AND GOVERNMENT

217. Indonesia. Departemen Penerangan. List of Publications issued by the Dept. of Information. Republic of Indonesia. Djakarta, Directorate of Publicity and Home Information, Dept. of Information, Republic of Indonesia, 1959?- v. (SA68-16701)

INFORMATION STORAGE AND RETRIEVAL SYSTEMS-- LAW

218. American Law Student Association. Techno-legal

Committee. A basic techno-legal bibliography for law students and young lawyers. Chicago, 1962. 11p. (63-4624)
Covers the information storage and retrieval systems concerned with the literature of the law.

219. Bigelow, Robert Pratt. Automation and law; a bibliography. 3d ed. Boston, 1965. 37p. (67-1567)
A short bibliography covering information storage and retrieval systems in the field of law and legal research.

INTERGOVERNMENTAL FISCAL RELATIONS--U.S.

220. Information Research Associates. Evidence and bibliography; 1969-1970 national collegiate debate topic. n.p., 1969. 70 ℓ. (73-13638)

THE INTERNATIONAL

221. Haupt, Georges. Program und Wirklichkeit; die internationale Sozialdemokratie vor 1914. Neuwied, Luchterhand, 1970. 253p. (77-508616)

INTERNATIONAL AGENCIES

222. Speeckaert, Georges Patrick. Bibliographie sélective sur l' organisation international. 1885-1964. Bruxelles, Union des associations internationales, 1965. 150p. (65-89502)

223. _____. International institutions and international organization; a select bibliography. Brussels, Publ. with assistance from UNESCO and in collaboration with the International Federation for Documentation, 1956. 116p. (57-837)

INTERNATIONAL LAW

224. Bibliography, 1915-1957, Quincy Wright, Professor of international law, emeritus, University of Chicago, visiting research scholar, Carnegie Endowment for International Peace, 1956-57. n.p., 1957. 40 ℓ. (NUC58-62)

225. Grotius Society, London, Library. Catalogue of the books in the library of the society. Arranged according to subjects by W.A. Bewes. London, Sweet & Maxwell, 1923. 63p. (24-9230)

226. Harvard University. Law School. Library. Catalog of international law and relations. Ed. by M. Moody. Cambridge, Mass., 1965-67. 20v. (65-23603)

227. al-Jam'īyah al-Misrīyah lil-Qānūn al-Duwalī. al-Maktabah. Catalog of the Library. Cairo, Egyptian Society of International Law, 1962. 52 ℓ. (76-21967)

228. Landheer, Bartholomeus. Fundamentals of public international law. Comp. with J.L.F. van Essen. Leyden, A.W. Sijthoff, 1953. 85p. (54-18291)

229. Pindić, Dimitrije. Bibliography of the selected articles on international public law published in Yugoslav and foreign periodicals covering the period 1955-1965. With T. Mitrović and P. Davinić. Beograd, Institut za medunarodnu politiku i privredu, Odeljenje za medunarodno pravo, 1968. 243p. (78-974065)

230. Robinson, Jacob. International law and organization. General sources of information. Leiden, A.W. Sijthoff, 1967. 560p. (67-25746)
    A good and extensive annotated bibliography on the subject.

231. Zile, Zigurds L. A guide to research in United Nations law. Madison, University of Wisconsin Law School, 1963. 39 ℓ. (NUC65-5600)

INTERNATIONAL ORGANIZATION

232. Aufricht, Hans. General bibliography on international organization and post-war reconstruction. New York, 1942. 28p. (NUCPre-1956Imprints)

233. ———. World organization, an annotated bibliography. 7th rev. ed. New York, Woodrow Wilson Memorial Library, 1946. 28p. (47-5741)

234. Documents of international organizations; a selected bibliography. Boston, World Peace Foundation, 1947-1950. 3 v. (49-1923rev)

235. Die Internationalen Wirtschaftsorganisationen im Schrifttum. Kiel, Bibliothek des Instituts für Weltwirtschaft, 1969- . v. (76-484614)
    Also includes materials on International economic relations.

236. Johnson, Harold S. International organization; a classified bibliography. With B. Singh. East Lansing, Asian Studies Center, Michigan State University, 1969. 261p. (79-630542)
    An extensive work with good coverage, and it also includes works on International relations.

237. Rogers, William Cecil. International administration; a bibliography. Chicago, Public Administration Service, 1945. 32p. (46-1182)

INTERNATIONAL RELATIONS

238. Carnegie Endowment for International Peace.

Current research in international affairs; a selected bibliography of work in progress by private research agencies in Australia, Canada, India, Pakistan, Union of South Africa, United Kingdom and the United States. New York, 1948- . v. (49-3920rev 2)

239. Foreign affairs bibliography; a selected and annotated list of books on international relations. 1919-32- . New York, Russell & Russell, 1960- . v. (60-11311)

240. Olivart, Ramón de Dalmau y de Olivart, marqués de. Bibliographie du droit international... Catalogue d'une bibliothèque de droit international et sciences auxiliaries. 2d ed. rev. et mise à jour. Paris, A. Pedone, 1905-10. 1278p. (5-34999)

241. U.S. Information Agency. International relations. Washington, U.S. Information Agency, Information Center Service, 1969. 45p. (76-602021)
    A general bibliography on international politics. Also includes some items of relevance to diplomacy.

242. U.S. Library of Congress. General Reference and Bibliography Division. A guide to bibliographic tools for research in foreign affairs. Comp. by H. F. Conover. 2d ed. with suppl. Westport, Conn., Greenwood Press, 1970. 145, 15p. (68-55129)
    A reprint of this important research tool.

243. United World Federalists. Panorama of recent books, films, and journals on world federation, the United Nations and world peace. Washington, 1960. 26 ℓ. (60-41459)

244. Zawodny, Janusz Kazimierz. Guide to the study of international relations. San Francisco, Chandler Pub. Co., 1965, c1966, 151p. (65-16765)

ITALY--COLONIES

245. Varley, Douglas Harold. A bibliography of Italian colonisation in Africa with a section on Abyssinia. Folkestone, Dawsons, 1970. 92p. (75-540436)
    A reprint with a new introduction of a 1936 publication.

JAPAN

246. Japan-Bibliographie. Hamburg, Düsseldorf, Deutsch-Japanisches Wirtschaftsbüro, 1968. 42p. (73-419732)

JAPAN--POLITICS AND GOVERNMENT

247. Ward, Robert Edward. A guide to Japanese reference and research materials in the field of Political Science. Ann Arbor, University of Michigan Press, 1950. 104p. (50-11597)

JAPANESE STUDIES

248. Shulman, Frank J. Japan and Korea; an annotated bibliography of doctoral dissertations in Western languages, 1877-1969. Comp. and ed. for the Center for Japanese Studies, University of Michigan. Chicago, American Library Association, 1970. 340p. (71-127675)

JUDGES--U. S.

249. Dahl, Richard C. The American judge, a bibliography. With C. E. Bolden. Vienna, Va., Coiner Publications, 1968. 330p. (68-2244)

250. Roper, D. Bibliography of Supreme Court Justices to 1963. n. p., 1963. 22 ℓ. (NUC69-60750)

JURISPRUDENCE

251. Dias, Reginald Walter Michael. A bibliography of jurisprudence. Being a companion to Jurisprudence, 2d ed., London, Butterworths, 1964. 234p. (64-55605)

KENNEDY, JOHN FITZGERALD, PRES. U.S., 1917-1963

252. Crown, James Tracy. The Kennedy literature: a bibliographical essay on John F. Kennedy. New York, New York University Press, 1968. 181p. (68-29428)

KENYA

253. Webster, John B. A bibliography on Kenya. With S. G. F. Kassam, R. S. Peckham and B. A. Skapa. Syracuse, N. Y., Program of Eastern African Studies, Syracuse University, 1967. 461p. (68-1122)

KOREA (DEMOCRATIC PEOPLE'S REPUBLIC)--POLITICS AND GOVERNMENT

254. Kyriak, Theodore E. North Korea, 1957-1961; a bibliography and guide to contents of a collection of United States Joint Publications Research Service translations on microfilm. Annapolis, Research & Microfilm Publications, 196-. 29p. (66-1213)
    Also covers Economic conditions and social conditions.

KOREAN WAR, 1950-1953

255. Park, Hong-Kyu. The Korean war; an annotated bibliography. Marshall, Tex., Demmer Co., 1971. 29p. (74-150826)

256. No item under this number

LABOUR PARTY (GT. BRIT.)

257. Labour Party (Gt. Brit.) Bibliography. London, Labour Party, 1967. 2, 96p. (68-78097)

LATIN AMERICA

258. Brodowski, Joyce H. Latin America today; a bibliography. 3d rev. ed. Trenton, N.J., State College, Roscoe L. West Library, 1966. 48 ℓ. (NUC67-5116)

259. Chilcote, Ronald H. Revolution and structural change in Latin America; a bibliography on ideology, development, and the radical left (1930-1965). Stanford, Calif., Hoover Institution on War, Revolution and Peace, Stanford University, 1970. 2v. (68-28100)

260. Gierth, Sieglinde. Veröffentlichungen über moderne Politik und Geschichte der iberoamerikanischen Länder; eine Auswahl deutscher und ausländischer Bücher und Artikel. Mit F. Herzog. Hamburg, Ibero-Amerika Haus, 1964. 42p. (70-219231)

261. McGill University, Montreal. French Canada Studies Programme. Bibliothèque. Le Canada français et l'Amérique latine; bibliographie. Comp. par P. Jetté et J.P. Jolin. Montréal, Bibliothèque, Centre d'études canadiennes-françaises, Université McGill, 1969. 13 ℓ. (78-20965)

262. Mason, Lois E., comp. Bibliography of Latin America, 1955-1964; books, monographs, periodicals, articles. Columbus, Dept. of Geography, Ohio State University, 1965. 232 ℓ. (65-64902)

Latin America

263. Sable, Martin Howard. <u>Latin-American studies in the non-Western World and Eastern Europe; a bibliography on Latin America in the languages of Africa, Asia, the Middle East, and Eastern Europe, with transliterations and translations in English,</u> Metuchen, N.J., Scarecrow Press, 1970. 701p. (73-13114)

264. Spell, Lota May (Harrigan). <u>Research materials for the study of Latin America at the University of Texas.</u> Westport, Conn., Greenwood Press, 1970, c1954. 107p. (71-144116)

265. U.S. Dept. of the Army. <u>Latin America and the Caribbean; analytical survey of literature.</u> Washington, U.S. Govt. Print. Off., 1969. 319p. (76-603569)

266. Weaver, Jerry L. <u>The political dimensions of rural development in Latin America: a selected bibliography. (1950-1967).</u> Long Beach, Calif., California State College, 1968, 92p. (NUC68-70931)

LATIN AMERICA--POLITICS AND GOVERNMENT

267. Brown, Lyle C. <u>A selected bibliography on Latin American government and politics.</u> Waco, Texas, Baylor University, 1963. 33 ℓ. (NUC65-42328)

LATVIA

268. Ozols, Selma Aleksandra. <u>Latvia: a selected bibliography.</u> Washington, K. Karusa, 1963. 144p. (63-21426)

LAW

269. Association of American Law Schools. <u>Law books</u>

Law

recommended for libraries. South Hackensack, N.J., F.B. Rothman, 1967-   . v. (67-30383)
> This service is a compilation of 46 subject lists which provide libraries with carefully selected and briefly annotated lists of law books which are recommended for libraries of various sizes. The six binders are updated regularly and the service is available on a subscription basis.

270. A Bibliography on foreign and comparative law: books and articles in English. Dobbs Ferry, N.Y., Published for the Parker School of Foreign and Comparative Law, Columbia University in the city of New York by Oceana Publications, 1790/1953-   . v. (55-11076 rev 3)

271. Coke, Sir Edward. A catalogue of the library of Sir Edward Coke. Ed. by W.O. Hassel. New Haven, Yale University Press, 1950. 98p. (50-11420)

272. Francisco, Vicente J. Legal bibliography. Manila, P.I., East Publishing, 1959. 354p.

273. Harvard University. Law School. Library. Annual legal bibliography. v. 1-   . 1960/61- . Cambridge, Mass. v. (61-18217)

274. ———— . Catalogue of the library of the Law school of Harvard University ... Cambridge, Mass., The Law School, 1909. 2v. (9-26645 rev.)

275. ———— . Publications, 1923-1959. By S. Glueck, R. Pound, Prof. of law, Harvard Law School, and E.T. Glueck, research associate in criminology, Harvard Law School; bibliography. Cambridge, Harvard Law School, 1959. 23 ℓ. (61-29069)

Law

276. Hicks, Frederick Charles. Materials and methods of legal research. 3d rev. ed. Rochester, N.Y., the Lawyers co-operative publishing company, 1942. 659p. (42-52177)
Also covers works dealing with the study and teaching of law, law libraries, and briefs.

277. Howell, Margaret A. A bibliography of bibliographies of legal material. Woodbridge, Printed by the New Jersey Appellate Print. Co., 1969. 2v. (76-8410)

278. International Association of Legal Science. A register of legal documentation in the world. 2d ed., rev. and enl. Prepared with the International Committee for Social Sciences Documentation. Paris, UNESCO, 1957. 423p. (52-3966)

279. Jacobstein, J. Myron. Recommended non-legal reference books for law libraries. New York, 1958. 4 ℓ. (NUC 58-62)

280. Lincoln's Inn, London. Library. A guide to Commonwealth law reports, legislation and journals in the Lincoln's Inn Library. 2d ed. Comp. by the authority of the Librarian by Y.H. McGowan. London, 1967. 79 ℓ. (70-506443)
Combined second edition of two earlier publications entitled: Guide to Commonwealth and colonial legislation, 1964, and Guide to Commonwealth and colonial law reports, 1965.

281. Lipen, Martin. Bibliotheca realis iuridica (post Friderici Gottlieb Struvii et Gottlob Augusti Jenichenii curas emendata) Hildesheim, New York, G. Olms, 1970. 5v. (73-543877)
Includes Roman law, and Canon law.

282. New York University. School of Law. Library.

A catalogue of the law collection at New York University, with selected annotations; comp. and ed. by J.J. Markle. New York, Law Center of New York University, 1953. 1372p. (53-6439)
Classified, with subject and author indexes. To be kept up to date with pocket supplements.

283. Oppenheim, Leonard. Materials on legal bibliography. New Orleans, Tulane Book Store, 1948. 79p. (48-25770)

284. Ordine avvocati e procuratori di Milano. Biblioteca. Dizionario bibliografico di opere giuridiche. Classificazione in ordine alfabetico per materie con sottoclassificazione cronologica e, per talune materie, sistematica delle opere della biblioteca dell'Ordine di Milano. A. cura di M. Rubino-Sammartano, con la collaborazione di A. Frontini, U. Caccia. Milano, A. Giuffrè, 1970. 262p. (70-531242)

285. Pålsson, Lennart. Bibliografisk introduktion til fremmed og komparativ ret. Bibliograpfisk introduktion til utländsk och komparativ rätt. With O. Lando. København, Ervervsøkonomisk Forlag (Harck), 1968. 309p. (71-371693)

286. Plucknett, Theodore Frank Thomas. Bibliography and legal history. (In the papers of the Bibliographic Society of America. Chicago, Ill., 1932. v. 26, pt. 1-2, 1932, p. 128-142) (CD33-5)

287. Quezon, Philippines. University of the Philippines. Library. Checklist of legal periodicals available in the Law Library. Comp. by M. Feliciano. Quezon City, Library of the University of the Philippines, 1963. 22 ℓ. (NUC65-56048)

288. Rajasthan, India. High Court of Judicature. Library. Catalogue of the Rajasthan High Court Library. Jaipur, Printed at Madhu Printers, 1968. 1 v. (72-908362)

289. Sydney. University. Law School. Library. List of serials held in Law School Library. Rev. ed. Sydney, 1968. 141 ℓ. (75-444183)

290. Vom Recht im Rheinland. Ausstellg. 22. April-20. Juli 1969. (Katalog v. Toni Diederich.) Köln, Kölnisches Stadtmuseum, 1969. 117p. (77-199493)

LAW--AFRICA, EAST

291. London. University. Restatement of African Law Project. Bibliography of African law. London, Restatement of African Law Project, School of Oriental and African Studies, University of London, 1961?- . v. (67-35282)

LAW--BELGIUM

292. Belgium. Parlement. Bibliothèque. Catalogue systematique de la Bibliothèque de la Chambre des représentants. New York, B. Franklin, 1969. 2 v. in 1. (68-57256)
    Covers social sciences and political science.

LAW--BULGARIA

293. Sipkov, Ivan. Legal sources and bibliography of Bulgaria. V. Gsovski, general editor. New York, Published for Free Europe Committee by F.A. Praeger, c1956. 199p. (57-13220)

LAW--CHINA

294. Bodde, Derk, comp. Chinese law; a selected bibliography of the communist period. By A. B. Clark. Cambridge, Mass., East Asia Research Center, 1961. 8 ℓ. (63-55301)

LAW--COMMONWEALTH OF NATIONS

295. London. University. Institute of Advanced Legal Studies. Union list of Commonwealth and South African law: a location guide to Commonwealth and South African legislation, law reports and digests held by libraries in the United Kingdom at May 1963. 1963 ed. London, 1963. 129p. (65-74924)

LAW--CZECHOSLOVAK REPUBLIC

296. Mid-European Law Project. Legal sources and bibliography of Czechoslovakia. By A. Bohmer and others. V. Gsovski, general editor. New York, Published for Free Europe Committee, by F. A. Praeger, 1959. 180p. (58-9696)

LAW--ECUADOR

297. Larrea Holguín, Juan Ignacio. Bibliografía jurídica del Ecuador. Quito, Edit. Casa de la Cultura Ecuatoriana, 1970. 178p. (79-544026)

LAW--ESTONIA

298. Mid-European Law Project. Legal sources and bibliography of the Baltic States (Estonia, Latvia, Lithuania) by J. Klesment and others. V. Gsovski, general editor. New York, Pub-

lished for Free Europe Committee, by Praeger, c1963. 197p. (63-15981)

LAW--EUROPE

299. London. University. Institute of Advanced Legal Studies. Union list of West European legal literature: publications held by libraries in Oxford, Cambridge and London. London, Institute of Advanced Legal Studies, 1966. 426p. (67-78488)

LAW--EUROPE, EASTERN

300. Bussmann, Christian. Bibliographie des deutschsprachigen Schrifttums zum Ostrecht. (1945-1964). With W. Durchlaub. Trittau, Scherbarth, 1969. 304p. (70-555063)

LAW--FRANCE

301. Dramard, Eugène. Bibliographie raisonnée du droit civil, comprenant les matières du code civil et des lois postérieures qui en formant le complément; accompagnée d'une table alphabétique des noms d'auteurs. Paris, Firmin-Didot et cie etc., 1879. 371p. (4-10277)

302. Grandin, A. Bibliographie générale des sciences juridiques, politiques, économiques et sociales de 1800 à 1925-1926. Publiée par la Société anonyme du Recueil Sirey ... Paris, Société anonyme du Recueil Sirey, L. Tenin, directeur, 1926. 3v. (27-15383)
    Covers political science, economics, and the social sciences.

303. Szladits, Charles. Guide to foreign legal materials: French, German, Swiss. New York, Published for the Parker School of Foreign

and Comparative Law, Columbia University, by Oceana Publications, 1959. 599p. (59-8608)

LAW--GT. BRIT.

304. Beale, Joseph Henry, comp. A bibliography of early English law books. Cambridge, Mass., Harvard University Press, 1926. 304p.
———. A supplement to Beale's Bibliography of early English law books. Comp. by Robert B. Anderson. Cambridge, Mass., Harvard University Press, 1943. 50p. (26-46217)

305. Cowley, John Duncan. A bibliography of abridgments, digests, dictionaries and indexes of English law to the year 1800. London, Quaritch, 1932. 196p. (32-16900)

306. A Legal bibliography of the British Commonwealth of Nations. London, Sweet & Maxwell, 1955- . v.

307. Manchester Incorporated Law Library Society. Catalogue of the books of the Manchester Incorporated Law Library Society. Manchester, 1935. 316p. (76-19881)

308. Sweet and Maxwell, ltd., London. Guide to law reports and statutes. 4th ed. London, 1962. 143p. (63-4500)

309. United Kingdom National Committee of Comparative Law. A bibliographical guide to the law of the United Kingdom, the Channel Islands and the Isle of Man. London, University of London, Institute of Advanced Legal Studies, 1956. 219p. (A57-3445)

LAW--HUNGARY

310. Mid-European Law Project. Legal sources and bibliography of Hungary, by A. K. Bedo and G. Torzsay-Biber; V. Gsovski, general editor. New York, Published for Free Europe Committee by F. A. Praeger, 1956. 157p. (56-13220)
Also covers legal sources in Transylvania.

LAW--INDIA

311. Alexandrowicz, Charles Henry. A bibliography of Indian law. Madras, New York, Indian Branch, Oxford University Press, 1958. 69p. (59-1923)

LAW--ISRAEL

312. Livneh, Ernst. Israel legal bibliography in European languages, with 1965 supplement. Jerusalem, Academon, 1965. 118p. (HE67-1642)

313. ———. Israel legal bibliography in European languages. Jerusalem, Mif'al hashichpul, The Hebrew University Students Press, 1963. 85p. (HE66-225)

LAW--ITALY

314. Grisoli, Angelo. Guide to foreign legal materials: Italian. Dobbs Ferry, N. Y., Published for the Parker School of Foreign and Comparative Law, Columbia University in the City of New York, by Oceana Publications, 1965. 272p. (65-5785)

LAW--JAPAN

315. Japan. Mombushō. Daigaku Gakujutsu-kyoku.

Bibliography of the studies on law and politics. 1952- . n.p. v. (59-54547)
English and Japanese.

LAW--LATIN AMERICA

316. American Association of Law Libraries. Committee on Foreign and International Law. Union list of basic Latin American legal materials. Ed. Kate Wallach. South Hackensack, N.J., Published for American Association of Law Libraries by F.B. Rothman, 1971. 64p. (70-145539)

LAW--OREGON

317. Beardsley, Arthur Sydney. Code making in early Oregon. Seattle, Wash., The University of Washington, 1936. 31p. (36-19660)

LAW--PERIODICALS--GT. BRIT.

318. London. University. Institute of Advanced Legal Studies. Union list of legal periodicals: a location guide to holdings of legal periodicals in libraries in the United Kingdom. 3rd ed. London, University of London (Institute of Advanced Legal Studies), 1968. 179p. (70-402220)

LAW--PERIODICALS--INDEXES

319. An Index to legal periodical literature... Boston, 1888-1926; Indianapolis, 1933- . v. (0-605 rev.)

320. Index to legal periodicals. Jan. 1926/Sept. 1928- . New York, Published for the American Association of Law Libraries by

the H.W. Wilson Co., 1929- . v. (41-21689)

321. Index to legal periodicals. v.1- . Jan, 1909- . New York City, Published for the American Association of law libraries by the H.W. Wilson Co., 1909- . v. (11-3276 rev. '41)

322. Union list of foreign legal periodicals of the Southwest Chapter of the American Association of Law Libraries. Comp. by G.F. Olivera. Austin, Tarlton Law Library, University of Texas, 1970. 76 ℓ. (73-632201)

LAW--PHILOSOPHY

323. Perticone, Giacomo. Filosofia del dritto e dello stato, Storia delle dottrine politiche, a cura de Rodolfo de Mattei. Roma, 1943. 190p.

LAW--POLAND

324. Mid-European Law Project. Legal sources and bibliography of Poland. By P. Siekanowicz. V. Gsovski, general editor. New York, published for Free Europe Committee, inc., by F.A. Praeger, 1964. 311p. (64-15524)

LAW--SCANDINAVIAN

325. Ginsburg, Ruth Bader. A selective survey of English language studies on Scandinavian law. So. Hackensack, N.J., F.B. Rothman, 1970. 53p. (77-118020)
    Covers only the essential items.

LAW--STUDY AND TEACHING

326. Texas. University. School of Law. Selected

bibliography on trends in legal education. Austin, 1968. 37 ℓ. (NUC69-138169)

LAW--SWEDEN

327. Cervin, Ulf. Gallringslista och förteckning över aktuell juridisk literatur. Hösten 1969. Utg. av. Bibliotekstjänst. Lund, Utgivaren; Solna, Seelig, 1970. 46p. (73-516911)

LAW--U. S.

328. American Bar Foundation. Index to legal theses and research projects. 1954- . Chicago. v. (54-14889 rev. 3)
 Also includes dissertations and research in jurisprudence.

329. American Bar Foundation. Cromwell Library. A checklist of American Bar Association general publications, with a supplement to the check list of section publications by V. L. Pederson. Chicago, American Bar Foundation, 1964. 112p. (65-725)

330. American Bar Foundation. Project on Unauthorized Practice of the Law. Unauthorized practice source book; a compilation of cases and commentary on unauthorized practice of the law. Rev. ed., by S.A. Bass. Chicago, American Bar Foundation, 1965. 206p. (65-28386)

331. Andrews, Joseph L. The law in the United States of America; a selective bibliographical guide. New York, New York University Press, 1966. 100p. (67-1256)
 This annotated bibliography provides listings of American codes, statutes, and court reports and their indexes and digests; brief analyses of the contents and relative

Law--U. S. 60

merits of important legal treatises and
text books; and a listing of the major
American legal periodicals, together with
price information.

332. Anglo-American law collections: University of
California Law Libraries Berkeley and Davis,
with Library of Congress class K added; combined catalog. Comp. and ed. by M. D.
Schwartz and D. F. Henke. South Hackensack,
N. J., F. B. Rothman, 1970. 10v. (79-
134436)

333. Beardsley, Arthur Sydney. Assignments to accompany the use of legal bibliography and the
use of law books. With O. C. Orman. 2d
ed. Brooklyn, Foundation Press, 1948. 128p.
(48-2330)

334. _____. Bibliography of selected materials relating to the legislation of the New Deal.
With O. C. Orman. Seattle, Wash., University book store, 1935. 111 ℓ. (35-8003)

335. _____. Legal bibliography and the use of law
books. With O. C. Orman. 2d ed. Advance
pamphlet. Brooklyn, Foundation Press, 1947.
172p. (47-7023)

336. _____. Manual of answers to accompany Legal bibliography and the use of law books.
Chicago, The Foundation Press, 1938. 106p.
(70-7000)

337. _____. Solutions to the Assignments to accompany Legal bibliography and the use of
law books. Chicago, The Foundation Press,
inc. 1940. 140p. (40-6999)

338. Jacobstein, J. Myron, ed. Law books in print.
With M. G. Pimsleur. South Hackensack,
N. J., Glanville Publishers, 1957. 384p.
(58-7619)

Law--U.S.

339. _____. _____. Consolidated ed. Dobbs Ferry, N.Y., Glanville Publishers, 1965. 2 v. (65-18284)

340. Keitt, Lawrence. An annotated bibliography of bibliographies of statutory materials of the United States. Cambridge, Harvard University Press, 1934. 191p. (34-11976)

341. London. University. Institute of Advanced Legal Studies. Union list of United States legal literature: holdings of legislation, law reports and digests of libraries in Oxford, Cambridge and London. 2d ed. London, 1967. 82p. (NUC67-101849)

342. Marke, Julius J., ed. Deans' list of recommended reading for prelaw and law students, selected by the deans and faculties of American law schools. New York, Oceana Publications, 1958. 178p. (57-14959)

343. Mersky, Roy M. Law books for non-law libraries and laymen; a bibliography. Comp. and ed. with annotations. Dobbs Ferry, N.Y., Oceana Publications, 1969. 110p. (69-15494)

> A convenient work for librarians untrained in legal bibliography. Includes a capsulated introduction to the intricacies and instrumentalities of legal research. Some areas are not treated adequately, but on the whole it gives good general coverage.

344. Michigan University. William L. Clements Library. Ius Americanum; examples of laws, treaties, jurisprudence, and legal documents found in the William L. Clements Library and selected for an exhibition in honor of the centennial of the University of Michigan Law School. Ann Arbor, 1959. 15p. (NUC58-62)

345. Notz, Rebecca Laurens (Love). Legal bibliog-

raphy and legal research. 3d ed. Chicago, Callaghan, 1952. 396p. (52-4884)

346. Pimsleur, Meira G. Checklists of basic American legal publications. South Hackensack, N.J., Published for American Association of Law Libraries by F.B. Rothman, 1962. 1v. (62-18944)

347. U.S. Dept. of the Interior. Library. Legal periodicals in the United States Department of the Interior Library. Compiled by Rebecca Fowler. Washington, U.S. Dept. of the Interior, Dept. Library, 1967. 17p. (68-60763)

LAW--WASHINGTON (STATE)

348. Beardsley, Arthur Sydney. The codes and code makers of Washington, 1889-1937. Seattle, Wash., University of Washington, 1939. 50p. (39-10417)

LAW--YUGOSLAVIA

349. Mid-European Law Project. Legal sources and bibliography of Yugoslavia. By F. Gjupanovich and A. Adamovitch. V. Gsovski, general editor. New York, Published for Free Europe Committee by F.A. Praeger, 1964. 353p. (64-15520)

LAW ENFORCEMENT--U.S.

350. Carpenter, Glenn B. Law enforcement training materials directory. Glenn Dale, Md., Capitol Press, 1969- . 1v. (75-83170)
    Covers materials on police training, and criminal investigation.

351. McGehee, A. Lee. Police literature: an annotated bibliography. Athens, Institute of Government, University of Georgia, 1970. 65p. (72-633912)

LEAGUE OF NATIONS

352. Aufricht, Hans. Guide to League of Nations publications; a bibliographical survey of the work of the League, 1920-1947. New York, Columbia University Press, 1951. 682p. (51-14811)

353. Breycha-Vanthier, Arthur Carl von. Sources of information; a handbook on the publications of the League of Nations. New York, Columbia University Press, 1939. 118p. (40-9850)

354. World Peace Foundation, Boston. Key to League of Nations documents placed on sale, 1920-1929. By Marie J. Carrol. Boston, World Peace Foundation, 1930. 340p.
_____. _____. Supplement. Boston, World Peace Foundation, 1931- . (4 supplements to 1936) (30-15910)

LEGAL SERVICE CORPORATIONS--U.S.

355. Kenyon, Carleton W. Law corporations; a bibliography on professional corporations and the Self-employed individuals tax retirement act. Sacramento, California State Library, Law Library, 1968? 18p. (76-631708)

LEGISLATION--LANCASHIRE, ENG.

356. Horrocks, Sidney, comp. Lancashire Acts of Parliament, 1266-1957. Manchester, Joint Committee on the Lancashire Bibliography, 1969. 350p. (70-516586)

LEGISLATIVE BODIES--U. S.

357. Michigan. State University, East Lansing. Institute for Community Development and Services. The Legislative process, a bibliography in legislative behavior. Comp. by the Michigan Senate fellows of 1963-64. East Lansing, 1963. 25p. (64-64642)

358. National association of state libraries. Public document clearing house committee. Checklist of legislative journals of states of the United States of America. Comp. by G. E. Macdonald. Providence, The Oxford Press, 1938. 274p. (38-38809)
  Includes materials on Government publications of the state governments, U. S. politics and government, and law in the U. S.

359. Pullen, William Russell. A checklist of legislative journals issued since 1937 by the states of the United States of America. Chicago, American Library Association, 1955. 59p. (55-8711)

LEGISLATIVE HEARINGS--U. S.

360. Andriot, Jeanne K. Checklist & index of Congressional hearings, 1958-1960. With J. L. Andriot. McLean, Va., Documents Index, 1967. 433p. (68-6189)

361. U. S. Congress. Senate. Library. Cumulative index of congressional committee hearings (not confidential in character) from Seventy-fourth Congress (January 3, 1935) through Eighty-fifth Congress (January 3, 1959) in the United States Senate Library. Indexed and compiled under the direction of F. M. Johnston, Secretary of the Senate, by R. D. Hupman, librarian and others. Washington, U. S. Govt. Print. Off., 1959. 823p. (59-61946)

LENIN, VLADIMIR IL'ICH, 1870-1924

362. Pelikán, Bohumil. Bibliografie bibliografií děl V.I. Lenina a literatura o Leninovi. K 100. výročí narození V.I. Lenina. With K. Kozelek. Praha, Ústav dějin socialismu, rozmn., 1970. 109p. (70-524739)

363. Zykmundová, Anna. K stému výročí narození V.I. Lenina. Výber nejnovější lit. Brno, Univ. knihovna, rozmn., 1970. 12p. (72-542195)

LIBERALISM

364. Camurani, Ercole. Contributo alla bibliografia del liberalismo nel mondo. Reggio Emilia, Partito liberale italiano, 1969. 111p. (70-560719)

LIBERTY OF SPEECH

365. Schroeder, Theodore Albert. Free speech bibliography; including every discovered attitude toward the problem covering every method of transmitting ideas and of abridging their promulgation upon every subject-matter. New York, B. Franklin, 1969. 247p. (79-84755)

LIBERTY OF THE PRESS

366. McCoy, Ralph Edward. Freedom of the press; an annotated bibliography. With a foreword by Robt. B. Downs. Carbondale, Southern Illinois University Press, 1968. 526p. (67-10032)
    Very extensive with good coverage.

LOCAL FINANCE--OREGON

367. Sewell, John. Financing State and local government in Oregon; a bibliography. Prepared in cooperation with the Bureau of Governmental Research and Service, University of Oregon, and the Oregon Council on Economic Education. Eugene?, Or., 1970. 52p. (75-633673)

LOCAL GOVERNMENT

368. Halász, D. Metropolis: a selected bibliography on administrative and other problems of metropolitan areas throughout the world ... The Hague, M. Nijhoff for the International Union of Local Authorities, 1961. 45p.

369. Mulhauser, Roland August, comp. A bibliography on regional government. With R.O. Huus. Cleveland, Publ. by the School of Applied Social Sciences with the Dept. of Political Science of Adelbert College of Western Reserve University, 1928. 59p. (28-20552 Rev.)

LOCAL GOVERNMENT--AFRICA, WEST

370. Ola, Israel Opeyemi. Local government in West Africa: an annotated bibliography. Ibadan, 1967. 193p. (NUC69-1779)

LOCAL GOVERNMENT--DENMARK

371. Skive kommunebibliotek. Kommunens styre og forvaltning. En litteraturfortegnelse. Skive, Skive Kommunebibliotek, Vestergade 1, 1970. 34p. (77-555310)

LOCAL GOVERNMENT--ITALY

372. Istituto per la scienza dell'amministrazione pubblica. Pubblicazioni. Contributi. 1- . Milano, etc., Giuffrè, etc., 1963- ι v. (72-406358)

LOCAL GOVERNMENT--NEW JERSEY

373. Messler Library. Documents of New Jersey local governments. Comp. and ed. by Catharine M. Fogarty. Rutherford, N.J., Fairleigh Dickinson University, 1967. 40p.
———— . ————. Supplement. no. 1- 1968- . Rutherford, N.J., no. (70-15832)

LOCAL GOVERNMENT--NEW YORK (STATE)

374. Parker, Ted F. Local government in New York State during the Dutch period; bibliography. Comp. with V.E. Parker. Albany, Government Affairs Foundation, 1968. 41p. (68-4788)

LOUISIANA--POLITICS AND GOVERNMENT

375. Public Affairs Research Council of Louisiana, inc. PAR index: a selective subject index of PAR research, 1951-1964. Baton Rouge, 1965. 56p. (NUC69-54030)

376. ————. A selective subject index: PAR research 1951-1960. Comp. by D.M. Beard, librarian. Baton Rouge, 1961.

MALAYSIA--POLITICS AND GOVERNMENT

377. Peritz, Rene. A selected bibliography of recent

works in English on political processes in Malaysia and Singapore, 1963-1968. Kingston, University of Rhode Island, 1969. 32 ℓ. (70-626055)

MANAGEMENT INFORMATION SYSTEMS

378. Ross, Joel E. An annotated bibliography of management information systems. With R. C. Murdick. Cleveland, Ohio, Association for Systems Management, 1970. 47p. (72-16121)

MAO TSÊ-TUNG, 1893-

379. Mao Tsê-tung. Mao papers, anthology and bibliography. Ed. by J. Ch'en. London, New York, Oxford University Press, 1970. 221p. (76-147091)

MARINE RESOURCES--LAW AND LEGISLATION

380. Koers, Albert W. The debate on the legal regime for the exploration and exploitation of ocean resources; a bibliography for the first decade, 1960-1970. Kingston?, R. I., 1970. 43 ℓ. (73-633189)

MARX, KARL, 1818-1883

381. Dortmund. Stadtbücherei. Karl Marx, 1818-1968: Mensch, Werk, Wirkung; Auswahl der neueren Literatur: Stadbücherei, Stadt- und Landesbibliothek, Institut für Zeitungsforschung, Dortmund. Bibliographische Bearbeitung: R. Ernemann. Herausgeber: Volksbüchereien der Freien Hansestadt Bremen. Bremen, 1968. 63p. (75-406218)

382. Rubel, Maxmilien. Bibliographie des oeuvres de Karl Marx; avec un appendice un répertoire des oeuvres de Friedrich Engles. Paris, M. Rivière, 1956. 272p. (A56-5592)

MARYLAND--POLITICS AND GOVERNMENT

383. Friedman, Robert S. A selected bibliography of Maryland state and local government. College Park, Bureau of Governmental Research, College of Business and Public Administration, University of Maryland, 1956. 120p. (56-63359)

MASS MEDIA

384. Mowlana, Hamid. International communications; a selected bibliography, 600 entries. Knoxville, School of Journalism, University of Tennessee, 1967. 38p. (77-2716)

MASSACHUSETTS--HISTORY--COLONIAL PERIOD

385. Whitmore, William Henry. A bibliographical sketch of the laws of Massachusetts colony from 1630-1686. Boston, Rockwell and Churchill, 1890. 150p. (4-8131)

MASSACHUSETTS--POLITICS AND GOVERNMENT

386. Goodwin, George, comp. A selected bibliography on Massachusetts politics and government. Amherst, Bureau of Govt. Research, University of Massachusetts, 1968. 34p. (71-625542)

MEDICAL JURISPRUDENCE

387. Brittain, Robert P. Bibliographie des travaux

français de médecine légale. With A. Saury and M.-R. Guidet. Préf. by Pr. Louis Roche. Paris, Masson, 1970. 188p. (73-515476)

388. Nick, William V. Index of legal medicine, 1940-1970; annotated bibliography. Columbus, Ohio, Legal Medicine Press, c1970. 694p. (71-148391)

METROPOLITAN GOVERNMENT

389. Livingston, David T., comp. Annotated bibliography, urban and suburban politics. n. p., 1961? 23 ℓ. (NUC66-87994)

MEXICO--GOVERNMENT PUBLICATIONS

390. Mesa, Rosa Quintero. Mexico. Ann Arbor, Mich., University Microfilms, 1970. 351, 4p. (72-121004)
    A union list of Mexican government publications and periodicals.

MEXICO--POLITICS AND GOVERNMENT

391. Johnson, Charles W. México en el siglo xx; una bibliografía social y política de publicaciones extranjeras, 1900-1969. México, Instituto de Investigaciones Sociales, 1969. 435p. (70-13724)
    Also includes materials concerning Mexican social conditions.

MICHIGAN--GOVERNORS

392. Michigan. State University of Agriculture and Applied Science, East Lansing. Institute for Community Development and Services. A se-

lected bibliography of biographical sources for the state governors of Michigan. Bibliographer: Gerard B. McCabe. East Lansing, Mich., 1959. 23 ℓ. (NUC58-62)

MICHIGAN--POLITICS AND GOVERNMENT

393. Press, Charles. Selected bibliography: Michigan government and politics. East Lansing, Institute for Community Development and Services, Michigan State University, 1963. 12 ℓ. (64-64639)

394. Turano, Peter J. Michigan State and local government and politics: a bibliography. Ann Arbor, Bureau of Government, Institute of Public Administration, University of Michigan, 1955. 269p. (56-13525)

MILITARY ART AND SCIENCE

395. American University, Washington, D.C. Special Operations Research Office. Annotated bibliography of SOLO publications. Washington, D.C., 1966. 32p. (NUC68-86237)

396. Becker, Fritz, bibliographer. Bibliographie: Deutscher Militärverlag. Berlin, Deutscher Militärverlag, 1962. 159p. (63-5416)

397. Riascos Sánchez, Blanca. Indice militar colombiano. Medellín, Editorial Universidad de Antioquia, 1968. 163 ℓ. (73-235023)

398. Zentralbibliothek der Bundeswehr. Militärwissenschaftliche Quellenkunde; Neuerwerbskatalog der Zentralbibliothek der Bundeswehr. Jahrg. 1- (Heft 1-); Jan./Feb. 1963- . Düsseldorf. v. (73-417214)

MILITARY HISTORY

399. Higham, Robin. Official histories; essays and bibliographies from around the world. Manhattan, Kansas State University Library, 1970. 644p. (74-634493)

MILL, JOHN STUART, 1806-1873

400. Mill, John Stuart. Bibliography of the published writings of John Stuart Mill. Ed. from his manuscript with corrections and notes by N. Macminn, J.R. Hainds, and J.M. McCrimmon. Evanston, Ill., Northwestern University, 1945. 101p. (45-5303)

MINORITIES--U.S.

401. Los Angeles. University of Southern California. Library. An introduction to materials for ethnic studies in the University of Southern California Library. Los Angeles, 1970. 196p. (76-278151)

402. U.S. Special Staff for Labor Relations and Equal Opportunity. Not just some of us; a limited bibliography on minority group relations. 2d ed. Baltimore, U.S. Social Security Administration, 1969. 42p. (70-608069)

403. Utah. State Board of Education. Minority groups; a bibliography. Salt Lake City, Office of the State Supt. of Public Instruction, 1968. (i.e. 1969) 20, 65p. (77-633380)

MISSISSIPPI--POLITICS AND GOVERNMENT

404. Mississippi. University. Bureau of Governmental Research. An annotated bibliography on Mississippi's economy, business, industry,

Missouri

and government, 1930-1963. University, University of Mississippi, 1964. 259p. (64-65139)

MISSOURI--GOVERNMENT PUBLICATIONS

405. Missouri State government documents. Jefferson City, Missouri State Library. no. in v. (76-629423)

MONROE DOCTRINE

406. Bradley, Phillips. A bibliography of the Monroe doctrine, 1919-1929. Letchworth, Printed by the Garden City Press; London, by the London School of Economics, 1929. 39p. (30-9506)

MUNICIPAL GOVERNMENT

407. Brooks, Robert Clarkson. A bibliography of municipal problems and city conditions. New York, Arno Press, 1970. 346p. (78-112527)

408. Los Angeles. Public Library. Municipal Reference Library. The government of metropolitan areas, a bibliography. Los Angeles, 1947. 43 ℓ. (48-25364)

MUNICIPAL GOVERNMENT--GT. BRIT.

409. Gross, Charles. A bibliography of British municipal history, including gilds and parliamentary representation. New York, London, Longmans, Green, 1897. 461p. (1-19965)

MUNICIPAL GOVERNMENT--ITALY

410. Lozzi, Carlo. Biblioteca istorica della autica e

nuova Italia; saggio di bibliografia, analitico, comparato e critico. Bologna, A. Forni, 1963. 2v. (NUC67-8178)
Also includes works on the history of Italy.

MUNICIPAL GOVERNMENT--U.S.

411. Government Affairs Foundation. Metropolitan communities: a bibliography with special emphasis upon government and politics. Chicago, Public Administration Service, 1957, c1956. 392p.

⎯⎯⎯⎯. ⎯⎯⎯⎯. Supplement. 1955-57- . Chicago, Public Administration Service. v. (56-13382)

412. Munro, William Bennett. A bibliography on municipal government in the United States. 2d ed. Cambridge, Harvard University Press, 1915. 472p. (16-1083)

MUNICIPAL GOVERNMENT BY CITY MANAGER

413. Booth, David Albin. Council-manager government, 1940-64: an annotated bibliography. Chicago, International City Managers' Association, 1965. 38p. (65-3964)

MUNICIPAL OFFICIALS AND EMPLOYEES--U.S.

414. Public Administration Service. Urban government manpower, a preliminary bibliography. Washington, Public Administration Service, 1961. 1v. (NUC67-61830)

NARCOTICS

415. Tompkins, Dorothy Louise (Campbell) Culver. Drug addiction: a bibliography. Berkeley,

University of California, Bureau of Public Administration, 1960. 130p. (61-62588)

NATIONAL INDUSTRIAL RECOVERY ACT

416. Beardsley, Arthur Sydney. A selected bibliography of legal and other materials relating to the National Industrial Recovery Act. New York, 1934. 15-31p. (34-21880)

NATIONALISM

417. Deutsch, Karl Wolfgang. Nationalism and national development; an interdisciplinary bibliography. With R. L. Merritt. Cambridge, Mass., MIT Press, 1970. 519p. (79-90750)

418. Pinson, Koppel Shub. A bibliographical introduction to nationalism. With a foreword by Carlton J.H. Hayes. New York, Columbia University Press, 1935. 70p. (35-11450)

NATIONALISM--AFRICA

419. Chilcote, Ronald H. Emerging nationalism in Portuguese Africa; a bibliography of documentary ephemera through 1965. Stanford, Calif., Hoover Institution on War, Revolution, and Peace, Stanford University, 1969. 114p. (68-8810)

NATURAL RESOURCES--PERIODICALS

420. Quebec (Province). Dept. of Natural Resources. Library. Répertoire des périodiques. Québec, 1969. 52p. (76-552131)

NEAR EAST

421. Fatemi, Ali Mohammad S. Political economy of the Middle East; a computerized guide to the literature. With A. Amirie and P. Kokoropoulos. Akron, Ohio, Dept. of Economics, University of Akron, 1970. 346, 326, 49p. (77-17252)
    Also covers north Africa.

422. Middle East Institute, Washington, D.C. Current research on the Middle East. 1955- . Washington. v. annual. (56-2109)

423. U.S. Dept. of State. Library Division. Point four: Near East and Africa; a selected bibliography of studies on economically underdeveloped countries. New York, Greenwood Press, 1969. 136p. (68-55124)
    Includes works on the economic conditions of the Near East and Africa.

NEW JERSEY. DEPT. OF COMMUNITY AFFAIRS

424. New Jersey. Dept. of Community Affairs. Publications of the New Jersey Department of Community Affairs. Trenton, 1968? 25 ℓ. (76-630954)

NEW MEXICO--POLITICS AND GOVERNMENT

425. Irion, Frederick Clarence. Selected and annotated bibliography on politics in New Mexico. 4th ed. Santa Fé, Legislative Council Service of New Mexico, 1959. 117 ℓ. (59-63371)

NIGERIA--GOVERNMENT PUBLICATIONS

426. U.S. Library of Congress. General Reference

and Bibliography Division. Nigerian official publications, 1869-1959; a guide. Compiled by Helen F. Conover. Washington, 1959. 153p. (59-60079)

NIGERIA--POLITICS AND GOVERNMENT

427. Murray, D.J. The progress of Nigerian public administration; a report on research. Comp. with J. Barbour and E.O. Kowe for the Institute of Administration, University of Ife, Nigeria. Ibadan, Institute of Administration, University of Ife, 1968. 238p. (71-16693)

NORTH ATLANTIC REGION

428. Conference on North Atlantic Community, Bruges, 1957. The Atlantic Community; an introductory bibliography. Leiden, A.W. Sythoff, 1961- . 2v. (loose-leaf) (62-39959)

NORTH ATLANTIC TREATY ORGANIZATION

429. North Atlantic Treaty Organization. Bibliographie. (Documentation établie par Madame J. Forget, chargée de la bibliothèque au Service de presse, avec le concours des délégations nationales et du Secrétariat) Paris, 1962. 165p. (65-53374)

430. ———. Bibliography. Paris, Nato-Otan, 1964. 205p. (65-37557)

431. ———. NATO bibliography... Paris, 195-? 44p. (NUC58-62)

432. U.S. Dept. of the Army. Nuclear Weapons and NATO; analytical survey of literature. Washington, 1970. 450p. (79-607373)

NORTH CAROLINA--POLITICS AND GOVERNMENT

433. Maybury, Catherine M. Publications of the Institute of Government, 1930-1956. Chapel Hill, 1957. 32 ℓ. (57-62843)

434. Palotai, Olga C. Publications of the Institute of Government, 1930-1962. Chapel Hill, Institute of Government, University of North Carolina, 1963? 78p. (64-63272)

NORWAY--GOVERNMENT PUBLICATIONS

435. Skarprud, Elsa. NATO. Stortingsdokumenter og et utvalg litteratur på norsk. Oslo, Nobelinstituttets bibliotek, 1967. 10 ℓ. (78-413444)
    Also covers Storting, Norway.

OHIO--GOVERNMENT PUBLICATIONS

436. Ohio. State Library, Columbus. Checklist publications of the State of Ohio, 1803-1952. Columbus, Ohio Library Foundation, 1964. 131p. (65-70943)

ORGANIZATION

437. Marquis, Stewart D. Bibliography on Systems. Rev. ed. East Lansing, Institute for Community Development and Services, Michigan State University, 1966. 18 ℓ. (64-64641)
    A list of selected books and articles on general systems and theory; human factors in systems; systems engineering; business and industrial; community; control; ecological information; service; and social, economic and political systems.

ORGANIZATION FOR EUROPEAN ECONOMIC COOPERATION

438. Organization for European Economic Cooperation. General catalogue of books published from 1948-1958. Paris, 1958. 109p. (NUC58-62)

ORGANIZATION OF AMERICAN STATES

439. Pan American Union. Columbus Memorial Library. Documentos oficiales de la Organización de los Estados Americanos. Indice y lista general. v.1- 1960- . Washington, Unión Panamericana. v. in (PA65-152)

ORIENTAL STUDIES

440. Cumulative bibliography of Asian studies, 1941-1965: author bibliography. Boston, Mass., G.K. Hall, 1969 (i.e. 1970) 4v. (79-12105)

PACIFISM

441. Miller, William Robert. Bibliography of books on war, pacifism, nonviolence, and related studies. Rev. ed., with addenda and author index. Nyack, N.Y., Fellowship of Reconciliation, 1961. 37p. (61-12678)

PAKISTAN

442. Abernethy, George L. Pakistan: a selected, annotated bibliography. 3d ed., rev. and enl. Vancouver, distributed by the Publications Centre, University of British Columbia, 1968. 56p. (78-458343)

PAKISTAN--POLITICS AND GOVERNMENT

443. Niaz, Mohammad Aslam. Public administration in Pakistan; a select bibliography. With A. M. Qureshi. Karachi, National Institute of Public Administration, 1966. 75p. (SA68-12766)

444. Rahman, M. A. Administrative reforms in Pakistan; an annotated bibliography. Lahore, Pakistan Administrative Staff College, 1969. 124p. (76-931000)

PARIS. PEACE CONFERENCE, 1919

445. Gunzenhäuser, Max. Die Pariser Friedenskonferenz 1919 und die Friedensverträge 1919-1920; Literaturbericht und Bibliographie. Frankfurt am Main, Bernard & Graefe, 1970. 287p. (76-526303)
    Includes works on treaties of the first world war.

PAROLE

446. Bates, Frederick L. Literature on parole. With R. Payne and F. K. Gibson. Rev. Athens, Institute of Government, University of Georgia, 1965. 67p. (66-65323)

447. Gibson, Frank Kenneth. Literature on parole. With R. Payne and F. L. Bates. 1967 ed. Athens, Institute of Government, University of Georgia, 1967. 95p. (68-64542)
    Brief but fair coverage.

PASSIVE RESISTANCE

448. Carter, April. Non-violent action; a selected bibliography. With D. Hoggett and A. Rob-

erts. Rev. and enl. ed. London, Housmans; Haverford, Pa., Center for Non-violent Conflict Resolution, Haverford College, 1970. 83p. (78-511821)
A general bibliography on passive resistance.

PEACE

449. Bibliographie zur Friedensforschung. Hrsg. von Gerta Scharffenorth und Wolfgang Huber. Unter Mitwirkung von J. Bopp et al. Mit einer Einführung von Gerta Scharffenorth. Stuttgart, E. Klett, c1970. 187p. (70-23938)
Also includes works on international relations and disarmament.

450. Gray, Charles Howard. A bibliography of peace research indexed by key words. With L. B. Gray and G. W. Gregory. Eugene, Or., General Research Analysis Methods, 1968. 164p. (68-3018)
Deals with the information storage and retrieval systems and the literature of peace and its subject headings.

451. Hague. Palace of Peace. Library. Catalogue. Par P.C. Molhuysen et E.R. Oppenheim. Leyde, A.W. Sijthoff, 1916. xivp., 2 ℓ., 5-1576 col.
. ... Premier supplément du Catalogue (1916) par P.C. Molhuysen et D. Alberts. Leyde, A.W. Sijthoff, 1922. xivp., 1 ℓ., 5-1042 col.
. ... Index alphabétique du Catalogue (1916) et du Supplément (1922). Leyde, A.W. Sijthoff, 1922. 2p., 1 ℓ., 9-790 col.
. ... Deuxième supplément (1929) au Catalogue (1916). Par J. ter Meulen et A. Lysen... Leyde, A.W. Sijthoff, 1913. xxp., 1 ℓ., 5-1554 col.

    ──────. ...Index alphabétique par noms d'auteurs ou mots d'ordre du Catalogue (1916) et des Suppléments (1922 et 1929). Leyde, A.W. Sijthoff, 1932. 2p. 1 ℓ., 9-1466 col.

    ──────. ...Index sommaire par ordre alphabétique des matières du Catalogue (1916) et des Suppléments (1922 et 1929). Leyde, A.W. Sijthoff, 1933 76 col.

    ──────. Catalogue de la bibliothèque du Palais de la paix: droit, relations internationales, histoire. Troisième supplément (1937) (Acquisitions: 1928/1929-1936). Par J. Ter Meulen et A. Lysen... Leyde, A.W. Sijthoff, 1937. xix, ii-xixp., 1 ℓ., 5-2742 col.

    ──────. ──────. ──────. Index alphabétique par noms propres du troisième supplément (1937) (Acquisitions: 1928/1929-1936) Leyde, A.W. Sijthoff, 1937. 79p. (19-20066)

    Also includes International law and relations.

452. ──────. Library of the Peace palace, documentation center: law and law reports, international relations, diplomatic history, peace movement. Leyden, A.W. Sijthoff's publishing company, 1938. 19p. (38-32763)

453. Pan American Union. Columbus Memorial Library. Bibliografia de las conferencias interamericanas. Washington, Departamento de Asunted culturales, Unias Pan-americana, 1954. 277p. (PA54-62)

454. Pickus, Robert. To end war: an introduction to the ideas, books, organizations, work, that can help. With R. Woito. 3d ed. Berkeley, Calif., World Without War Council, 1970. 261p. (75-15051)

    Covers international relations as well as the subject of peace.

PENNSYLVANIA--POLITICS AND GOVERNMENT

455. Branning, Rosalind Lorraine. Annotated bibliography on Pennsylvania State Government. Prepared for the Dept. of Political Science, University of Pittsburgh. Pittsburgh, 1959. 42p. (59-15270)
    Supplement to Bibliography on Pennsylvania Government, issued in 1941.

PERSONNEL MANAGEMENT

456. Michigan. State Library, Lansing. Public administration bibliography. Lansing, 1966. 4p. (67-63387)
    A brief listing of works on personnel management.

457. U. S. Civil Service Commission. Library. Personnel policies and practices. Washington, 1970. 106p. (73-609016)
    Deals with personnel management within the U. S. Civil Service.

POLITICAL PARTIES--CANADA

458. McGill University, Montreal. French Canadian Studies Programme. Canadian political parties, 1791-1867; 1867- (including books, review articles, graduate theses, and pamphlets). Montreal, 1966? 70 ℓ. (68-6258)

POLITICAL PARTIES--FRANCE

459. Charlot, Jean. Répertoire des publications des partis politiques français, 1944-1967. A catalogue of the publications of the French political parties, 1944-1967. Paris, A. Colin, 1970. 245p. (73-562312)

POLITICAL PARTIES--LATIN AMERICA

460. Kantor, Harry. Latin American political parties; a bibliography. With the staff of the University of Florida Program in the Comparative Study of Latin American Political Parties. Gainesville, Reference and Bibliography Dept., University of Florida Libraries, 1968. 113p. (A68-7771)

461. Wheeler, Lora Jeanne, comp. Latin American political parties: a bibliography. n. p., 1966. 97 ℓ. (NUC68-107702)

POLITICAL PARTIES--U. S.

462. Garrison, Lloyd W., comp. American politics and elections; selected abstracts of periodical literature, 1964-1968. Assistant: K. M. Curran. Santa Barbara, Calif., ABC-Clio, 1968. 45p. (68-58982)
    Also includes works on voting and U. S. presidents.

463. Jones, Charles O. The role of political parties in Congress; a bibliography and research guide. With R. B. Ripley. Tucson, Published for the Institute of Government Research by the University of Arizona Press, 1966. 41p. (66-63498)

464. New York Public Library. Political parties in the United States, 1800-1914; a list of references. New York, New York Public Library, 1915. 74p.

465. U. S. Library of Congress. Division of Bibliography. Brief list of books on political parties before 1865. Washington, 1921. 4p.

466. ―――. List of references on party government. Washington, 1920. 6p.

467. ———. List of references on the national committees of political parties. Washington, 1924. 7p.

468. ———. List of works relating to political parties in the United States. Washington, Govt. Print. Off., 1907. 29p. (7-3506)

469. ———. Selected list of references on the convention system. Washington, 1927. 8p.

470. ———. Short list of references to recent writings on American politics and political parties. Washington, 1925. 3p.

471. Wynar, Lubomyr Roman. American political parties; a selective guide to parties and movements of the 20th century. Littleton, Colo., Libraries Unlimited, 1969. 427p. (75-96954)
    An extensive bibliography on modern American political parties.

POLITICAL SCIENCE

472. ABC pol sci; advance bibliography of contents: political science and government. v.1- Mar. 1969- . Santa Barbara, Calif., ABC-Clio. v. (70-6512)
    A service which reproduces the tables of contents of approximately 260 journals in the social sciences with emphasis upon political science.

473. Adam, Melchior. Vitae Germanorum jureconsultorum et Politicorum: qvi superiori seculo, et quod excurrit, floruerunt. Concinnatae a Melchiore Adamo. Cum indice triplici, personarum gemino, tertio rerum. Haidelbergae, Impensis heredum J. Rosae, excudit Johannes Georgius Geyder, 1620. 16p., 488p.

An early bibliography dealing with both political science and law.

474. American political science review; cumulative index to v. 1-57: 1906-1963. Ed. by Kenneth Janda. Evanston, Ill., Northwestern University Press, c1964. 224, 27p. (8-9025)
    A computerized bibliography of this important political journal.

475. Baker, George Hall, ed. Bibliography of political science, 1887. Boston, New York, Ginn, 1887. 56p. (1-18155)

476. Basic source materials in political science. Ed. by Robert B. Harmon. San Jose, Calif., Dibco Press, etc., 1969- . v. (68-28325)
    A series of selected and annotated bibliographies designed to aid in researching and understanding the complex world of politics.

477. Bibliography for the Honour school of philosophy, politics and economics. Oxford, Blackwell's, 1937. 36p. (39-31954)

478. Bibliography in politics, for the Honour school of philosophy, politics and economics. Drawn up by Professor Headlam-Morley and others. Oxford, Blackwell, 1949. 55p. (50-3098)

479. Beittel, William. Inter-university research program in institution building: bibliography. Pittsburgh, Graduate School of Public and International Affairs, University of Pittsburgh, 196-? 1v. (loose leaf) (NUC67-3439)
    A loose leaf bibliography dealing with organization in general along with economics, political science and social change.

480. Bowker, Richard Rogers, ed. The reader's guide in economic, social and political sci-

ence, being a classified bibliography, American English, French and German, with descriptive notes, author, title and subject index, courses of reading, college courses etc. Edited with George Iles. New York, The Society for Political Education, 1891. 169p. (Z-105)

481. Bozza, Tommaso. Scrittori politici italiani dal 1550-al 1650, saggio di bibliografia. Roma, Edizioni di "Storia e letteratura," 1949. 218p. (A51-3260)

482. Brindley, Mary Elizabeth. A study of the Columbia university library's acquisitions in political science and government from 1930-1935 inclusive. 1937? 24 ℓ.

483. British Library of Political and Economic Science. London. Bulletin of the British library of political and economic sciences. London, 1913-33. 6v. (21-3572 rev. 2)

484. ———. Guide to the collections. London, 1948. 136p. (50-4479)

485. Brock, Clifton. A guide to library resources for political science students at the University of North Carolina. Chapel Hill, University of North Carolina Library, 1965. 69p. (67-64368)

486. ———. The literature of political science; a guide for students, librarians, and teachers. New York, Bowker, 1969. 232p. (79-79426) An excellent guide for students doing research in the field. Includes over 500 annotated entries plus information on U.S. government and U.N. documents. Also contains helps on library usage and social science research aids.

487. Brookings Institution, Washington, D.C. Pub-

Political Science 88

lications of the staff, 1952 to 1960. Washington, 1960. 36p. (60-53526)
Also includes economics.

488. Burchfield, Laverne. Student's guide to materials in political science. Prepared under the direction of the Sub-committee on research of the Committee on policy of the American Political Science Association. New York, Holt, c1935. 426p. (35-15776)

489. Columbia University. Faculty of political science. A bibliography of the Faculty of political science of Columbia University, 1880-1930. New York, Columbia University Press, 1931. 365p. (31-11485)

490. Eaton, Andrew Jackson. Current political science publications in five Chicago libraries; a study of coverage, duplication and ommission ... n.p., 1946. 212p. (A46-2981)

491. Galloway, George Barnes. American pamphlet literature of public affairs (a descriptive list of current pamphlet series). Washington, D.C., National Economic and Planning Association, 1937. 16p. (SD38-8)
Includes works on social science, economics, U.S. politics and government as well as political science.

492. Gard, Richard Abbott. Buddhist political thought; a bibliography. (Outlines and bibliographical index, SAIS, summer session, 1952.) Washington, School of Advanced International Studies, 1952. 73 ℓ. (54-35907)

493. Harmon, Robert Bartlett. A bibliography of bibliographies in political science. 1st ed. San Jose, Calif., Dibco Press, 1964. 16 ℓ. (NUC67-20787)

494. _____. Political science; a bibliographical

Political Science

guide to the literature. New York, Scarecrow Press, 1965. 388p.
―――― . Supplement, 1968. Metuchen, N.J., Scarecrow Press, 1968. 331p. (65-13557rev)

495. ―――― . A selected guide to annotated sources in political science. San Jose, Calif., Bibliographic Information Center for the Study of Political Science, 1970. 24 ℓ. (71-117410)

496. ―――― . Sources and problems of bibliography in political science. San Jose, Calif., Dibco Press, 1966. 73p. (66-18521)

497. ―――― . Suggestions for a basic political science library; a guide to the building of a political science collection for school, classroom or individual. San Jose, Calif., Bibliographical Information Center for the Study of Political Science, 1970. 35p. (75-117411)
An annotated listing of 101 basic works in the field suggested as starters for building a political science collection.

498. Historical association, London. Bibliography of political theory... London, The Historical Association, 1916. 8p. (A35-246)

499. Holland, Henry M. A checklist of paper-back books and reprints in political science. Washington, D.C., The American Political Science Association, 1962. 47p. (NUC67-36343)

500. International bibliography of political science. Bibliographie internationale de science politique. v.1- 1953- . Paris, UNESCO v. (54-14355)

501. International political science abstracts. Documentation politique international. v.1- 1951- . Paris. v. (54-3623)

Abstracts are in English or French and
are selected from a large number of periodicals published in various countries.
Arrangement varies. Recent issues are
classified by large categories, with cumulated annual author and subject indexes.

502. Lancaster, Lucy Lee. A list of books in sociology and political science to be purchased with $1,000 to supplement the titles suggested by the Shaw list in these fields. 1931? 26p.

503. Levine, Robert Alan. A bibliography on political anthropology. With G. Roth. Evanston, 1964? 71p. (NUC 65-77306)

504. McCulloch, John Ramsay. The literature of political economy; a classified catalogue of select publications in the different departments of that science, with historical, critical, and biographical notices. New York, A. M. Kelley, bookseller, 1964. 407p. (63-22258)

505. McDougall, Donald. Catalogue of books in all the libraries on the theory and practice of politics. West Ham, Public Libraries, 1935. 127p.

506. Maier, Hans, bibliographer. Politische Ideen in der freien Welt; eine einführende Bibliographie. Unter Mitwirkung von Wanda v. Baeyer, et al. Hrsg. von der Arbeitsgemeinschaft Der Bürger im Staat. Stuttgart, W. Kohlhammer, 1959. 60p. (60-28505)

507. Maryland. University. Bureau of Governmental Research. Political science; a selected bibliography of books in print, with annotations. Compiled by F. L. Burdette, director, J. N. Willmore, and J. V. Witherspoon. College Park, 1961. 97 ℓ. (61-64130)

508. Matczak, Sebastian A. Philosophy; a select,

classified bibliography of ethics, economics, law, politics, sociology. Louvain, Belgium, Editions Nauwelaerts, 1970. 308p. (79-80677)
Covers some items of political science.

509. Mattei, Rodolfo de. ...La storia delle dottrine politiche. Firenze, G.C. Sansoni, 1938. 173p. (A42-1881)

510. Meyriat, Jean, ed. La science politique en France, 1945-1958; bibliographie commentée. Oeuvre collective par M. Maume. Pref. de Jacques Chapsal. Paris, Fondation nationale des sciences politiques, 1960. 134p. (64-56138)

511. Mohl, Robert von. Die Geschichte und Literatur der Staatswissenschaften, in Monographien dargestellt. Graz, Akademische Druck- u. Verlagsanstalt, 1960. 3v. (63-30146)
An extensive history of the literature of political and social science. Bibliography is included either in footnotes or within the text. Includes a bibliographic index in the third volume (pp. 733-832).

512. Naude, Gabriel. Bibliographia politica. Venetiis, F. Baba, 1633. Torino, Bottega d'Erasmo, 1961. 1p., 2-115 columns. (NUC63-52199)

513. Pogány, András H. Political science and international relations; books recommended for the use of American Catholic college and university libraries. With H.L. Pogány. Metuchen, N.J., Scarecrow Press, 1967. 387p. (67-10196)

514. Princeton University, Library. Class of '83 library of political science and jurisprudence. Finding list. Princeton, N.J., 1893. 44p. (2-166)

Political Science 92

515. Schautz, Jane. <u>Life, liberty, and law, a bibliography of political science books for young adults.</u> Illustrations by Sister M. Cor Immaculatum. Scranton, Pa., Dept. of Librarianship, Marywood College, 1967. 53p. (NUC69-100280)

516. Shurter, Edwin DuBois. <u>Both sides of 100 questions briefly debated, with affirmative and negative references.</u> New York, Noble and Noble, 1925. 265p. (26-10764)
   Includes references on economics, social sciences, and U.S. politics and government.

517. Universal Reference System. <u>Political science, government & public policy series.</u> Princeton, N.J., Princeton Research Pub. Co., 1965-69. 10v. (78-6367)
   Perhaps the most extensive current source for materials in the field.

518. Virginia. State Library, Richmond. <u>Finding list of the social sciences, political science, law, and education.</u> (In its Bulletin. Richmond, 1910. v. 3, no. 1, 2 and 3, pp. 3-352; Classed catalog with author title and subject index) (10-23427)

519. Washington University, St. Louis, Libraries. <u>Guide to research material in political science.</u> By J.M. Thom. St. Louis, 1952. 2pts. (A55-3924)

520. Wisconsin. University. Dept. of Political Science. <u>Library resources for political science in Milwaukee with selected bibliographies by Pearl Robertson and Vito Vardys.</u> Milwaukee, 1958. 138 ℓ. (NUC58-62)

POLITICAL SCIENCE--BIBLIOGRAPHY--CATALOG

521. Harvard University. Library. <u>Government:</u>

classification schedule, classified listing by call number, author and title listing, chronological listing. Cambridge, Mass., Distributed by the Harvard University Press, 1969. 263p. (68-8886)
The classed list of the Widener Library of Harvard University in political science.

522. Wynar, Lubomyr R. Social sciences general references; political science, a selective and annotated bibliographical guide. Boulder, Social Sciences Library, University of Colorado Libraries, 1962. 66, ix ℓ. (63-62700)

POLITICAL SCIENCE--BIBLIOGRAPHY--PERIODICALS

523. Quarterly check-list of economics & political science. Darien, Conn. (etc.), American Bibliographic Service. v. in (64-56101)
Began publication with Mar. 1958 issue.

POLITICAL SCIENCE--INDIA

524. Gautam, Brijendra Pratap. Researches in political-science in India; a detailed bibliography. With a foreword by A.V. Rao. Kanpur, Oriental Pub. House, 1965. 116p. (SA67-2611)

POLITICAL SCIENCE RESEARCH

525. Cornog, Geoffrey Yates. University research in government; projects in process, October, 1968. Athens, Published for the Conference of University Bureaus of Governmental Research by the Institute of Government, University of Georgia, 1968. 73p. (72-626881)
Includes materials on political science in general and public administration in particular.

Pollution 94

526. Dennis, Jack Stanley. Recent research on political socialization; a bibliography of published, forthcoming, and unpublished works, theses, and dissertations, and a survey of projects in progress. With the assistance of I. H. Bromall and others. Prepared for the Theory and Research Working Committee on Political Socialization of the Council on Civic Education, Lincoln Filene Center for Citizenship and Public Affairs, Tufts University. Medford, Mass., 1967. 66 ℓ. (NUC69-7288)

527. Rachavan, Susheila. Anthropology in government, an analytical bibliography. Washington, D.C., Bureau of Social Science Research, 1967. 44 ℓ. (NUC69-900)
Includes materials on ethnology.

POLLUTION--U.S.--BIBLIOGRAPHY--CATALOGS

528. Indiana. University. Library. Government Publications Dept. Man and his environment; selected Government publications, 1950-1970. Bloomington, 1970. 95 ℓ. (79-632886)

POOR--U.S.

529. Institute for Rural America. Poverty, rural poverty and minority groups living in rural poverty: an annotated bibliography. With Spindletop Research. Lexington, Ky., Spindletop Research, 1969. 159p. (70-272648)

530. Tompkins, Dorothy Louise (Campbell) Culver. Poverty in the United States during the sixties; a bibliography. Berkeley, Institute of Governmental Studies, University of California, 1970. 542p. (74-632910)
Includes materials on economic assistance in the U.S.

531. U. S. Social Security Administration. Office of Research and Statistics. Poverty studies in the sixties; a selected, annotated bibliography. Washington, U. S. Govt. Print. Off., 1970. 126p. (78-605471)

POUND, ROSCOE, 1870-

532. Harvard University. Law School. Library. A bibliography of the writings of Roscoe Pound, 1940-1960. By George A. Strait, assistant librarian. Cambridge, Mass., 1960. 52p. (61-3928)

533. Setaro, Franklyn Christopher. A bibliography of the writings of Roscoe Pound. Cambridge, Mass., Harvard University Press, 1942. 193p. (A42-638)

PRESIDENTS--U. S.--ELECTION

534. Szekely, Kalman S. Electoral college; a selective annotated bibliography. With a foreword by W. O. Reichert. Littleton, Colo., Libraries Unlimited, 1970. 125p. (79-136256)

535. Tompkins, Dorothy Louise (Campbell) Culver. Presidential succession; a bibliography. Rev. Berkeley, Institute of Government Studies, University of California, 1965. 29p. (66-63309)

536. U. S. Library of Congress. General Reference and Bibliography Division. Presidential inaugurations; a selected list of references. Rev. ed. Washington, 1960. 72p. (60-60085)

PROPAGANDA

537. Lasswell, Harold Dwight. Propaganda and pro-

motional activities; an annotated bibliography. Ed. with R.D. Casey and B.L. Smith. Chicago, University of Chicago Press, 1969. 450p. (75-77979)
   Includes works on publicity and public relations.

538. Smith, Chitra M. International communication and political warfare, an annotated bibliography. With B. Winograd and A.R. Jwaideh. 23 October 1952. Santa Monica, Calif., Rand Corp., 1952. 508p. (53-15568)
   Also includes works on public opinion and public relations.

PSYCHOLOGICAL WARFARE

539. U.S. Dept. of State. External Research Staff. A background reading list on psychological operations with special emphasis on Communist China. Washington, 1964. 26p. (64-62347)

PUBLIC ADMINISTRATION

540. Boston University. African Studies Program. Bibliographie sélective des livres, articles, et documentations traitant le sujet des problèmes administratifs africains. A selective bibliography of books, articles, and documents on the subject of African administrative problems. Prepared by Wilbert J. LeMelle. Boston, 1964. 51 ℓ. (79-7813)
   Includes books in both English and French. Special emphasis has been placed on the states of former French Africa.

541. _____. Bibliographie sélective d'ouvrages de langue français traitant des problèmes gouvernementaux et administratifs, notamment en Afrique. Select bibliography of French lan-

guage works in governmental and administrative problems, with special attention to Africa. Boston, 1963. 36 ℓ. (66-35192)

542. Cornell University. Graduate School of Business and Public Administration. <u>Basic library in public administration.</u> Ithaca, 1956. 59p. (NUC58-62)

543. _____. . <u>Management; a subject listing of recommended books, pamphlets and journals.</u> By Betsy Ann Olive, librarian. Ithaca, N.Y., 1965. 222p. (66-3708)
Also includes some works on economics.

544. <u>Current research projects in public administration</u> ... Chicago, etc. v. annual. (43-17005rev)
Began publication in 1938.

545. DeGrazia, Alfred. <u>Human relations in public administration; an annotated bibliography from the fields of anthropology, industrial management, political science, psychology, public administration, and sociology.</u> Chicago, Public Administration Service, 1949. 52p. (49-5538)

546. Denmark. Arbejds-, familie- og socialministeriernes bibliotek. <u>Bøger og tidsskrifter i det administrative bibliotek.</u> København K, Eksp.: Slotsholmsgade 12, 1967. 33 ℓ. (68-115040)

547. Institute of Public Administration, New York. <u>A bibliography of public administration.</u> By Sarah Greer, librarian of National Institute of Public Administration and New York Bureau of Municipal Research. New York City, National Institute of Public Administration, 1926. 238p. (26-6747)

548. _____. _____. New York City, Institute

of Public Administration, Columbia University, 1933- . v. (33-16617)
Also includes works on political science, social sciences, municipal government.

549. Liège, Université. Institut de sociologie. Bibliografie voor het overheidsbeheer. Liège, Administratien-universiteit, 1967. 105p. (68-78216)
Includes works on management.

550. ———. Bibliographie de l'administration publique. Une sélection d'ouvrages commentés par l'Institut de sociologie de l'Université de Liège à la demande de l'Institut Administration-Université. Liège, Institut de sociologie de l'Université de Liège, 1966. 101p. (67-92890)

551. ———. ———. 2de édition. Liège, Institut de sociologie de l'Université de Liège, 1968. 99p. (68-95149)

552. Mars, David. Suggested library in public administration: with 1964 supplement. With H. G. Frederickson. Los Angeles, International Public Administration Center, School of Public Administration, University of Southern California, 1964. 203p. (66-65279)

553. Michigan. University. Bureau of Industrial Relations. A selected list of books and periodicals in the field of personnel administration and labor-management relations. Ann Arbor, Mich., Graduate School of Business Administration, 1964. 26p. (65-63075)

554. Michigan. University. Institute of Public Administration. Comparative public administration: a selective annotated bibliography. 2d ed. By Ferrel Heady and Sybil L. Stokes. Ann Arbor, 1960. 98p. (60-64086)

Public Administration

555. Miley, Arthur L. Directory of planning, budgeting and control information. Oxford, Ohio, Planning Executives Institute, 1969. 142p. (70-20262)

556. New York State Library, Albany. Legislative Reference Library. Source material for the study of public administration. Albany, 1958- . v. (A59-9117)

557. Niaz, Mohammad Aslam. Organization & methods; an annotated select bibliography. With A.M. Qureshi. Karachi, National Institute of Public Administration, 1966. 26p. (SA68-4870)

558. Public Administration Service. Public Automated Systems Service. The computer in the public service: an annotated bibliography, 1966-1969. Chicago, Public Administration Service, 1970. 74p. (70-108757)

559. Public Personnel Association. A basic bibliography in public personnel administration; a general reference source for the personnel practitioner, the public administrator, the teacher, and the student. Chicago, 1961. 232-248p. (NUC58-62)

560. Recent publications on governmental problems. Chicago. v. weekly. (46-42921rev)

561. Seckler-Hudson, Catheryn. Bibliography on public administration, annotated. 4th ed. Washington, American University Press, 1953. 131p. (53-11892)
    Also includes works on U.S. politics and government.

562. Special Libraries Association. Social Science Group. Source materials in public administration, selected bibliography reprinted from public administration libraries (PAS publica-

tion no. 102). Chicago, Public Administration Service, 1948. 30p. (49-617)

563. Spitz, Allan A. Developmental change; an annotated bibliography. Lexington, University Press of Kentucky, 1969. 316p. (69-19766)
Covers the subjects of economic development, public administration and underdeveloped areas.

564. United Nations. Technical Assistance Administration. International bibliography of public administration. Bibliographie internationale de l'administration publique. Bibliografia internacional de administracion publica. New York, United Nations, 1957. 101p. (59-1040)

565. U.S. Veterans Administration. Medical and General Reference Library. Executive leadership in the public service; an annotated list of selected monographs. Rev. Washington, 1969. 23p. (70-601900)
Also includes works on management.

PUBLIC ADMINISTRATION RESEARCH

566. Cornog, Geoffrey Yates. University research in government, projects in process, 1966. Comp. with J. Oliver Green. Athens, Published for the Conference of University Bureaus of Governmental Research, American Society for Public Administration by the Institute of Government, University of Georgia, 1966. 99p. (67-66027)

PUBLIC OPINION

567. Bureau of Social Science Research, Washington, D.C. International communication and political opinion; a guide to the literature. By

Bruce Lannes Smith and C. M. Smith. Prepared for the Rand Corporation by the Bureau of Social Science Research Washington, D.C. Princeton, N.J., Princeton University Press, c1956. 325p. (56-10829)

568. Childs, Harwood Lawrence. A reference guide to the study of public opinion. Princeton, N.J., Princeton University Press, 1934. 105p. (34-38328)

PUBLIC OPINION POLLS

569. Rokkan, Stein. Comparative survey analysis; an annotated bibliography. With J. Viet. Paris, International Committee for Social Sciences Documentation, 1962. 62 ℓ. (67-112573)

PUBLIC RELATIONS--POLICE

570. Hewitt, William H., comp. Police-community relations: an anthology and bibliography. With C.L. Newman. Mineola, N.Y., Foundation Press, 1970. 360p. (72-123372)

RECOGNITION (INTERNATIONAL LAW)

572. Landheer, Bartholomeus. Recognition in international law. Comp. with J.L.F. van Essen. Leyden, A.S. Sijthoff, 1954. 28p. (54-39741)

REGIONAL PLANNING

573. Boston University. Area Development Center. New England development bibliography. Washington, U.S. Dept. of Commerce. Office of Regional Economic Development; U.S. Govt. Print. Off., 1966. 437p. (66-62057)

574. Connecticut. Office of State Planning. Regional planning publications in Connecticut; bibliography. Rev. Hartford, 1970. 61p. (77-633861)

575. Hamilton, F. E. Ian. Regional economic analysis in Britain and the Commonwealth: a bibliographic guide. London, Weidenfeld and Nicolson, 1969. 410p. (77-455452)

576. Minnesota. University. Public Administration Center. Inventory of research resources concerning a state-wide planning program for Minnesota. Prepared by the Public Administration Center of the University of Minnesota for the Minnesota Dept. of Business Development. Minneapolis, 1964. 64 ℓ. (66-64616)

577. Tarozzi, Ermanno. Elementi per una bibliografia sui temi dello sviluppo economico, sociale e territoriale con particolare riguardo all 'Emilia Romagna. A cura di Ermanno Tarozzi, Francesco Bonazzi Del Poggetto. Presentazione dell'on. Rino Nanni. Bologna, STEB, 1969. 66p. (77-538506)
    Also includes works on economic and social conditions of Emilia-Romagna.

578. Zawadzki, Stanislaw Maciej. Planowanie regionalne: bibliografia piśmiennictwa polskiego, 1945-1965: wybór. Warszawa, 1969. 318p. (73-245229)

REVOLUTIONS

579. Groth, Alexander. Revolution and elite access: some hypotheses on aspects of political change. Introd. by G. Roth. Davis, Institute of Governmental Affairs, University of California, 1966. 72p. (66-64510)

RIOTS--U.S.

580. McCarthy, Betty Anne. Riots and demonstrations; a selected bibliography. Sacramento, California, State Library, Law Library, 1969. 5p. (NUC69-113933)

581. U.S. National Clearinghouse for Mental Health Information. Bibliography on the urban crisis; the behavioral, psychological, and sociological aspects of the urban crisis. Prepared by the National Clearinghouse for Mental Health Information, Office of Communications, NIMH, and the Planning Branch, Office of Program Planning and Evaluation, NIMH. Chevy Chase, Md., National Institute of Mental Health, 1968. 158p. (77-600665)
    Includes works on Negroes and U.S. social conditions.

RUSSIA

582. Horecky, Paul Louis. Basic Russian publications; an annotated bibliography on Russia and the Soviet Union. Contributors: R.V. Allen and others. Chicago, University of Chicago Press, 1962. 313p. (62-20022)

583. Kyriak, Theodore E. Soviet Union: a bibliography. no. 1-3-July-Sept. 1962- . Annapolis, Research Microfilms. v. (62-20263)

584. Loventhal, Milton. The U.S.S.R., a selected bibliography: 1917-1956. San Diego, Calif. 1957. 42 ℓ. (NUC53-57)

585. U.S. Dept. of the Army. USSR: strategic survey; a bibliography. 1969 ed. Washington, 1969. 237p. (77-601689)
    Includes works on Russian politics and government.

RUSSIA--ARMED FORCES

586. Parrish, Michael. The Soviet armed forces books in English, 1950-1967. Stanford, Calif., Stanford University, Hoover Institution Press, 1970. 128p. (71-128167)

587. U.S. Dept. of the Army. Army Library. Soviet military power. Bibliography. New York, Greenwood Press, 1969. 186p. (78-90731)
    Includes works on Russian military policy.

RUSSIA--FOREIGN RELATIONS

588. Clemens, Walter C. Soviet disarmament policy, 1917-1963: an annotated bibliography of Soviet and Western sources. Stanford, Calif., Hoover Institution on War, Revolution and Peace, Stanford University, 1965. 151p. (65-12623)

RWANDA--POLITICS AND GOVERNMENT

589. Willot, Paul. Complément à la bibliographie rwandaise: disciplines du développement. Préf. de M. Walraet. n.p., Editions rwandaises, 1968. 51p. (73-541805)
    Also includes works on the economic and social conditions of Rwanda.

SCIENCE AND CIVILIZATION

590. Caldwell, Lynton Keith. Science, technology, and public policy; a selected and annotated bibliography. Assisted by W.B. DeVille and H.L. Shuchman. Bloomington, Indiana University, 1968- . v. (76-625128)

SCIENCE AND STATE--CANADA

591. National Science Library. Scientific policy, research and development in Canada; a bibliography. Ottawa, 1968. 72 ℓ. (75-486379)

SCIENCE AND STATE--U.S.

592. U.S. Library of Congress. Legislative Reference Service. Science, technology, and American diplomacy; a selected, annotated bibliography of articles, books, documents, periodicals, and reference guides. Prepared for the Subcommittee on National Security Policy and Scientific Developments of the Committee on Foreign Affairs, U.S. House of Representatives by the Science Policy Research and Foreign Affairs Divisions, Legislative Reference Service, Library of Congress. Comp. by G.J. Knezo, research associate. Washington, U.S. Govt. Print. Off., 1970. 69p. (77-606721)

SIMULATION METHODS

593. Roeckelein, Jon E. Simulation of organizations: an annotated bibliography. Alexandria, Va., George Washington University, Human Resources Research Office, 1967. 56p. (68-60760)

SOCIAL CHANGE

594. Brode, John. The process of modernization; an annotated bibliography on the sociocultural aspects of development. Foreword by A. Inkeles. Cambridge, Mass., Harvard University Press, 1969. 378p. (69-13765)
    This bibliography is intended to provide a tool with which scholars the world over

can sort out for their respective purposes
the vast literature pertaining to modernization.

595. Geiger, H. Kent. National development, 1776-
1966; a selective and annotated guide to the
most important articles in English. Metuchen,
N.J., Scarecrow Press, 1969. 247p. (77-
5813)

SOCIAL CLASSES

596. Glenn, Norval D. Social stratification: a research bibliography. With J.P. Alston and
D. Weiner. Berkeley, Calif., The Glendessary Press, 1970. 466p. (74-104325)

SOCIAL HISTORY

597. International Labor Office. Central Library and
Documentation Branch. Subject guide to publications of the International Labour Office,
1919-1964. Geneva, 1967. 478p. (79-
243089)
Also includes works on economic history.

SOCIAL PROBLEMS

598. Paisley, William J. Sources of information on
social issues: education, employment, public
health and safety, population, etc.; a brief
guide for journalists and others. Stanford,
Calif., 1969. 31p. (74-606486)

SOCIAL SCIENCE RESEARCH

599. Bibliography of published reports on TCR/ORA-
sponsored research. Rev. n.p., 1964.
9 ℓ. (79-415799)

SOCIAL SCIENCE RESEARCH--U.S.

600. North American Congress on Latin America.
NACLA research methodology guide. New
York, 1970. 72p. (76-15255)

SOCIAL SCIENCES

601. Adler, Catherine E. M. Social studies; an annotated list of recent books on politics, sociology, economics, international relations and world affairs for the use of librarians, teachers, adult students, students in universities and technical colleges and sixth forms in schools. London, School Library Association, 1965. 36p. (66-1113)

602. The American behavioral scientist. The ABS guide to recent publications in the social and behavioral sciences. New York, 1965. 781p. (65-17168)
A cumulation of annotations and citations which appeared in New Studies. Annotations are usually evaluative.

603. Association for Education in Citizenship. Bibliography of social studies; a list of books for schools and adults. London, Oxford University Press, 1936. xi, iii, 1p. (37-4720)

604. Augustus M. Kelley (Firm). Reprints; economic and allied social science classics. New York, 1969? 162p. (71-16598)

605. Barnes, Harry Elmer, ed. Contemporary social theory. With H. Becker and F.B. Becker. New York, Russell & Russell, 1971, c1940. 947p. (70-139899)

606. Barros, Maria Nazareth M. M. de. Introduçao aos estudos históricos e sociais; planos de aula. Belém, Curso de Biblioteconomia, 1967. 47p. (73-414011)

A brief bibliography dealing with the social sciences in general.

607. Bibliographia sociologica. Sociologie et droit. Sozial-wissenschaft und recht. Sociology and law. Sommaire méthodique des traites et revues. Bruxelles, Larcier, 1895. 2pt. in 1 v. (4-12058)

608. Boehm, Eric H. Blueprint for bibliography; a system for the social sciences and humanities. Santa Barbara, Calif., Clio Press, 1965. 22p. (65-25556)

609. Boston Public Library. A list of books on social reform in the public library of the city of Boston. Boston, The Trustees, 1898. 58p. (Z-189)

610. Bronnen voor literatuuronderzoek Samengesteld in opdracht van de Gemeenschappelijke Opleidingscommissie van het Nederlands Instituut voor Informatie, Documentatie en Registratuur, de Nederlandse Vereniging van Bibliothecarissen, de Nederlandse Vereniging van Bedrijfsarchivarissen. 4e geheel herz. uitg. Eindredaktie: G.M. van Andel, C. Coosen en W.C. 't Hart. 's-Gravenhage, De Gemeenschappelijke Opleidingscommissie (Burgemeester van Karnebeeklaan 19), 1968. 214p. (78-496016)
    Includes reference books, and science and technology.

611. Budapest. Magyar Közgazdaságtudományi Egyetem. A Marx Koróly Közgazdaságtudományi Egyetem oktatóinak szakirodalmi munkássága, 1945-1968; bibliográfia. Szerkeszto: M. László. Budapest, 1968. 436p. (72-234634)

612. Clarke, Jack Alden. Research materials in the social sciences. 2d ed. Madison, University

of Wisconsin Press, 1967. 56p. (67-25948)

613. Corbin, Doris. Open literature publications of the Social Science Department: 1966-1969. Santa Monica, Calif., Rand Corp., 1970. 96p. (70-278155)
Also includes works on world politics from 1945 on.

614. Desrochers, Edmond. Référence et bibliographie en sciences. Montréal, École de bibliotheconomie, 1967? v. (68-117855)

615. Gardin, Natacha. Applications des calculateurs aux sciences humaines, essai de présentation documentaire. Applications of computers in human sciences, essay of documentary presentation... Paris, Maison des sciences de l'homme, Centre de calcul et service d'échange d'informations scientifiques, 1968? lv. (76-400268)

616. Germany (Federal Republic, 1949-   ). Bundesministerium für Wirtschaft. Bibliothek. Verzeichnis der in der Bibliothek des Bundesministeriums für Wirtschaft vorhandenen Gutachten. Mit einem Vorwort von E. Richter. Bonn, 1965. 142p. (77-246357)

617. Hale, Barbara M. The subject bibliography of the social sciences and humanities. Oxford, New York, Pergamon Press, 1970. 149p. (78-113358)

618. Hanna, Paul Robert. An exhibit and bibliography of current and supplementary materials on social, economic, and political problems. n.p., 1934. 27p.

619. Hoffman, Bernard G. Tentative check list of social science periodicals and monograph series published in the United States and Canada. Washington?, 1961. 21 ℓ. (62-51540)

620. Hoselitz, Berthold Frank, ed. A reader's guide to the social sciences. With chapters by P. M. Blau and others. Rev. ed. New York, Free Press, 1970. 425p. (71-15373)

621. Interamerican Children's Institute. Library. Bibliografía sobre "El aumento de la población y su incidencia sobre la infancia, la adolescencia, la juventud y la familia americana." Montevideo, Instituto Interamericano del Niño, 1968. 92p. (75-240000)

622. International Committee for Social Sciences Documentation. A bibliography on the problem of change of scale in the social sciences. Classified and annotated by J. Meynaud. Paris, 1957. 46p. (58-22503)

623. Kronenberg, Henry Harold. Pamphlets on public affairs for use in social studies classes. With R. M. Tryon and H. E. Nutter. Cambridge, Mass., Distributed by the National Council for the Social Studies, 1937. 80p. (37-12782)

624. Kyriak, Theodore E. Catalog cards in book form for United States Joint Publications Research Service translations. Annapolis, Research & Microfilm Publications. v. in (63-14379)
    Began publication with issue for 1957/61.

625. Leamer, Laurence E. Suggestions for a basic economic library; a guide to the building of an economic library for school, classroom, or individual. With P. L. Guyton. Rev. New York, Joint Council on Economic Education, 1965. 58p. (65-4695)

626. Leipziger Kommissions- und Grossbuchhandel. Fachgruppenkatalog: Gesellschaftswissenschaften. Leipzig, 1964- . v. (74-242849)

Social Sciences

627. Lewis, Peter R. The literature of the social sciences; an introductory survey and guide. London, Library Association, 1960. 222p. (60-3467)

628. Literatur-Verzeichnis der politischen Wissenschaften. 1952- . München. v. (55-31220)

629. A London bibliography of the social sciences, being the subject catalogue of the British library of political and economic science at the School of Economics, the Goldsmiths' library of economic literature at the University of London, the libraries of the Royal anthropological institute, and certain special collections at University College, London, and elsewhere. Compiled under the direction of B. M. Headicar and C. Fuller with an introd. by S. Webb (Lord Passfield) ... London, The London School of Economics and Political Science, 1931-32. 4 v.
...Supplement... 1st- Containing the additions to the libraries named above. 1929- . Comp. under the direction of the librarian of the British library of political and economic science, by M. Plant. London, The London School of Economics & Political Science, 1934- . v. (31-9970)

630. Mason, John Brown. Research resources; annotated guide to the social sciences. Santa Barbara, Calif., ABC-Clio, 1968- . v. (68-9685)
An extensive annotated list of over 1200 reference sources in the social sciences. Volume 1 contains reference sources in international relations and recent history.

631. Needham, Christopher Donald. The study of subject bibliography with special reference to the social sciences. Assisted by E. Her-

man. College Park, School of Library and Information Services, University of Maryland, 1970. 221p. (75-630095)

632. Netherlands (Kingdom, 1815-   ). Central Bureau voor de Statistiek. <u>Bibliographie van regionale onderzoekingen op sociaalwetenschappelijk terrein.</u> Alfabetisch register 1946-1968. Met de namen van de provincies, gebieden, gemeenten, en plaatsen waarom trent in de tot dusverre verschenen uitgaven van de bibliographie literatuur is vermeld. 1. Algemene literatuur en grotere landsdelen. 2. Provicies en gebieden binnen iedere provincie. 3. Gemeente en plaatsen. 's-Gravenhage, Staatsuitgeverij, 1969. 35p. <u>_____. _____. Supplement 1968.</u> 's-Gravenhage, Staatsuitgeverij, 1969. 59p. (75-435686)

633. <u>Neue politische Literatur;</u> Berichte über das internationale Schrifttum. 1-   Jahrg.: Juli 1956- . Stuttgart, Ring-Verlag. v. (58-37179)

634. <u>New Studies:</u> a guide to recent publications in the social and behavioral sciences. New York, American Behavioral Scientist, n.d. v.

> A separate listing which also appears in the middle section of the <u>American Behavioral Scientist.</u> Includes full bibliographical citations, and annotations are brief with some being evaluative.

635. New York State Library, Albany. <u>Checklist of books and pamphlets in the social sciences; including anthropology, economics, philosophy, political science, psychology, welfare but not including education, history and law.</u> Albany, 1956. 142p. (A56-9307)

636. Public Affairs Information Service. <u>Bulletin</u>...

annual cumulation. 1st. - 1915- . New
York, 1915- . v. (16-920rev)
  Includes works on social sciences, political
  science and legislation.

637. Samford, Clarence D. Social studies bibliography: curriculum and methodology. Carbondale, Southern Illinois University Press, 1959. 101p. (59-13123)

638. Senn, Peter R. A short guide to the literature of the social sciences. With M. Senn. Boulder, Colo., Social Science Education Consortium, 1968. 53 ℓ. (79-5563)

639. Slavens, Thomas P., comp. Information sources in the social sciences. Ann Arbor, Campus Publishers, 1969. 1v.
  A classified listing of social science reference sources. Coverage is limited; however, annotations are excellent.

640. Social science abstracts. v.1-4, v.5, no. 1; Mar. 1929-Jan. 1933. Menasha, Wis., 1929-1933. 5v. (30-29596)

641. Social sciences and humanities index. New York, H.W. Wilson, 1916- . v. (16-21641rev 21)

642. Stammhammer, Josef. Bibliographie der socialpolitik. Jena, G. Fischer, 1896-1912. 2v. (1-6030)

643. Sumner, William Graham. Political economy and political science. A price and classified list of books recommended for general reading and as an introduction to special study. New York, The Society for Political Education, 1884. 36p. (8-7628)

644. Thompson, Olive. A guide to readings in civic education. Rev. and enl. Berkeley, Univer-

sity of California Press, 1924. 140p. (24-6454)

645. United Nations Educational, Scientific and Cultural Organization. Theses in the social sciences; an international analytical catalogue of unpublished doctorate theses, 1940-1950. 236p. (52-4847)

646. U. S. Dept. of State. External Research Staff. Political behavior. 2d ed. Washington, 1963. 60p. (64-61052)
Also includes materials on world politics.

647. Wynar, Lubomyr Roman. Guide to reference materials in political science; a selective bibliography. With L. Fystrom. Denver, Colorado Bibliographic Institute, 1966- . v. (66-1321)

SOCIAL SCIENCES--PERIODICALS--BIBLIOGRAPHY--CATALOGS

648. Belgium. Ministère des finances. Bibliothèque centrale. Catalogue des périodiques à la Bibliothèque centrale du Ministère des Finances. Catalogus der tijdschriften van de Centrale Bibliotheck van het Ministerie van Financiën. Bruxelles, Ministère des Finances, Bibliothèque Centrale, rue de la Loi, 14, 1969. 162p. (76-505689)

SOCIAL SCIENCES--PERIODICALS--BIBLIOGRAPHY--UNION LISTS

649. A Union catalogue of Western social science periodicals, held by 31 major libraries in Korea. Seoul, Social Sciences Documentation Centre, Yonsei University library, 1962. 60 ℓ. (70-281653)

SOCIAL SURVEYS

650. National Opinion Research Center. NORC social research, 1941-1964; an inventory of studies and publications in social research. Edited and annotated by J.M. Allswang and P. Bova. Chicago, 1964. 80p. (65-910)

SOCIAL WELFARE

651. Lopez, Manuel D. A guide to the literature of social welfare. Buffalo, Reference Dept., Lockwood Memorial Library and the School of Social Welfare, State University of New York at Buffalo, 1969? 24p.

SOCIALISM

652. Dolléans, Édouard. Mouvements ouvrier et socialiste, chronologie et bibliographie: Angleterre, France, Allemagne, États-Unis (1750-1818). With M. Crozier. Paris, Éditions ouvrières, 1950. 381p. (A51-4871)
    Covers labor and laboring classes, trade unions, and social reform also.

653. Egbert, Donald Drew. Socialism and American life. Edited with S. Persons. Princeton, N.J., Princeton University Press, 1952. 2v. (52-5828)

654. Goldwater, Walter. Radical periodicals in America, 1890-1950; a bibliography with brief notes. With a genealogical chart and a concise lexicon of the groups which issued them. New Haven, Yale University Library, 1964. 51p. (64-6244)

655. International socialist bibliography. v.1- Jan. 9, 1954- . London, Socialist International. v. in (60-39003)

656. Stammhammer, Josef. Bibliographie des Socialismus und Communismus. Jena, G. Fischer, 1893-1909. 3v. (1-6031)

SOCIALISM, CHRISTIAN

657. Ligthart Schenk, A. H. Bibliografie van het christen- en religieus-socialisme in Nederland, 1900-1940. n. p., 1969. 72p. (76-496289)

SOCIALIST LABOR PARTY--HISTORY--SOURCES

658. Socialist Labor Party. Records of the Socialist Labor Party of America: guide to a microfilm edition. F. Gerald Ham, editor. C. S. Warmbrodt and J. L. Harper, associate editors. L. E. Steinberg, manuscripts preparator. Madison, State Historical Society of Wisconsin, 1970. 28p. (79-19173)

SOCIOLOGICAL JURISPRUDENCE

659. Chambliss, William J. Sociology of the law: a research bibliography. With R. B. Seidman and A. Warden. Berkeley, Calif., Glendessary Press, 1970. 113p. (73-140068)

SOMALILAND--GOVERNMENT PUBLICATIONS

660. U. S. Library of Congress. General Reference and Bibliography Division. Official publications of Somaliland, 1941-1959; a guide. Compiled by Helen F. Conover. Washington, 1960. 41p. (60-60050)

SOUTH ASIA

661. South Asia: a bibliography for undergraduate li-

braries. By Louis A. Jacob and others.
Williamsport, Pa., Bro-Dart Pub. Co., 1970.
103p. (71-124578)

SOUTH ASIA--POLITICS

662. Menge, Paul E. Government administration in South Asia; a bibliography. Washington, Comparative Administration Group, American Society for Public Administration, 1968. 100p. (68-59108)

SOUTH DAKOTA--GOVERNMENT PUBLICATIONS

663. South Dakota. State Legislative Research Council. Bibliography of South Dakota State Legislative Research Council publications, July 1, 1951, through July 31, 1965; staff memorandum. Pierre, 1965. 18p. (79-631093)

664. ———. Bibliography of South Dakota State Legislative Research Council publications, July 1, 1951, through February 23, 1968: staff memorandum. Pierre, 1968. 24p. (68-66805)

SPACE LAW

665. Worldwide bibliography of space law and related matters. Bibliographie mondiale de droit spatial et matières connexes. Paris, International Institute of Space Law, 1964- . no. (76-237436)
   A continuing bibliography on this developing aspect of law.

SPANISH AMERICA

666. Bayitch, S.A. Latin America; a bibliographical

Spinoza, Benedictus De   118

   guide to economy, history, law, politics, and society. Coral Gables, Fla., University of Miami Press; distributed by Oceana Publications, New York, 1961. 335p. (60-53473)

667. Pan American Union. Columbus Memorial Library. Bibliography on public administration in Latin America. 2d ed., compiled by J. Grossmann, cataloger. Washington, Dept. of Cultural Affairs, Pan American Union, 1958. 198p. (PA58-33)

SPINOZA, BENEDICTUS DE, 1632-1677

668. Oko, Adolph S. The Spinoza bibliography. Published under the auspices of the Columbia University Libraries. Boston, G.K. Hall, 1964. 700p. (A65-685)

STATE GOVERNMENTS

669. Boston University. Bureau of Public Administration. Bibliography on state and local government in New England. Boston, 1952. 233p. (53-3433)

670. Graves, William Brooke. American state government and administration; a state by state bibliography of significant general and special works. Comp. with N.J. Small and E.F. Dowell. Chicago, Council of State Governments, 1949. 79p. (49-48663)

671. Herndon, James. A selected bibliography of materials in State government and politics. With O.P. Williams and C. Press. Lexington, Bureau of Government Research, University of Kentucky, 1963. 143p. (65-63255)

672. Press, Charles. State manuals, blue books, and election results. With O. Williams. Berke-

ley, Institute of Governmental Studies, University of California, 1962. 101p. (63-63225)

673. Tompkins, Dorothy Louise (Campbell) Culver. State government and administration; a bibliography. Berkeley, Bureau of Public Administration, University of California, 1955, c1954. 269p. (55-10467)

STATES, NEW--POLITICS

674. Carnell, Francis. The politics of the new states; a select annotated bibliography with special reference to the Commonwealth. London, Published for the Institute of Commonwealth Studies by Oxford University Press, 1961. 171p. (62-213)

STRIKES AND LOCKOUTS--CIVIL SERVICE

675. California. University. Institute of Governmental Studies. Strikes by public employees and professional personnel; a bibliography. Compiled by Dorothy C. Tompkins. Berkeley, 1967. 92p. (67-65515)

SWEDEN--POLITICS AND GOVERNMENT

676. Wallmén, Olof. Orientering i samhällsfrågor. Handledning i att söka fakta och förslag till litteratur. Lund, Bibliotekstjänst, Solna. Seelig, 1969. 106p. (73-555328)
Also includes works on Swedish social conditions.

TANZANIA--POLITICS AND GOVERNMENT

677. Decalo, Samuel. Tanzania: an introductory bib-

liography. Kingston?, University of Rhode
Island, 1968. 57 ℓ. (68-4789)

TAXATION

678. Harvard University. International Program in
Taxation. Bibliography on taxation in underdeveloped countries. Cambridge, Law School
of Harvard University, 1962. 75p. (62-
17751)

TELEVISION IN POLITICS

679. Television Information Office, New York. Library. Television in government and politics,
a bibliography. New York, Television Information Office, 1964. 62p. (64-6762)

TEXAS--POLITICS AND GOVERNMENT

680. Texas. University. Institute of Public Affairs.
Bibliography on Texas government. Rev. ed.
Austin, 1964. 194p. (64-64899)

THAILAND

681. Bitz, Ira. A bibliography of English-language
source materials on Thailand in the humanities, social sciences, and physical sciences.
Washington, Center for Research in Social
Systems, American University, 1968. 272p.
(79-22047)

TOTALITARIANISM

682. Freedom Institute, Iowa Wesleyan College. Freedom Institute bibliography. Mount Pleasant,
Iowa, 1969. 56p. (72-14502)

Covers items on totalitariansim, communism and dogmatism.

TRANSPORTATION--U.S.

683. Flood, Kenneth U. Research in transportation: legal/legislative and economic sources and procedure. Detroit, Gale Research Co., c1970. 126p. (72-118792)

684. Stover, John F. Transportation in American history. Washington, American Historical Association, 1970. 38p. (79-143196)

TREATIES

685. Harvard University. Law School. Library. Index to multilateral treaties; a chronological list of multi-party international agreements from the sixteenth century through 1963, with citations to their text. V. Mostecky, editor. F.R. Doyle, assistant editor. Cambridge, Mass.; distributed by Oceana Publications, Dobbs Ferry, N.Y., 1965. 301p. (65-29763)

TREATIES--COLLECTIONS

686. United Nations. Office of Legal Affairs. List of treaty collections. New York, 1956. 174p. (NUC53-7)

TURKEY--FOREIGN RELATIONS

687. Tamkoc, Metin. A bibliography on the foreign relations of the Republic of Turkey, 1919-1967, and brief bibliographies of Turkish statesmen. Ankara, Idari Ilimler Facültesi, Orta Doğu Teknik Universidesi, 1968. 248p. (NUC69-128721)

Turkey 122

TURKEY--RURAL CONDITIONS

688. Beeley, Brian W. Rural Turkey: a bibliographic introduction. Ankara, Hacettepe University, Institute of Population Studies, 1969. 120p. (72-256019)

TURKEY--SOCIAL CONDITIONS

689. Suzuki, Peter T. Social change in Turkey since 1950; a bibliography of 866 publications. Heidelberg, High Speed Press Center, 1969. 108p. (70-495419)

UNDERDEVELOPED AREAS

690. Akademie der Wissenschaften, Berlin. Institut für Wirtschaftswissenschaften. Bibliothek. Bürgerliche Theorien über unterent-wickelte Länder: internationale Auswahl-bibliographie. Auswertungszeitraum: ca. 1950 bis Juni 1960. Berlin, 1960? 185 ℓ. (74-255305)

691. Canadian Council for International Co-operation. Bibliography of international development. Ottawa, 1969. 28 ℓ. (76-474758)

692. Entwicklungsländer-Studien. Bd. 1- Bonn, Deutsche Stiftung für Entwicklungsländer, 1966- . v. (71-413524)

693. Frey, Frederick W. Survey research on comparative social change: a bibliography. With P. Stephenson and K.A. Smith, and with the assistance of the staff of the Human Factors in Modernization Project, Center for International Studies, M.I.T. Cambridge, Mass., MIT Press, 1969. 1v. (71-76449)

694. Havana. Biblioteca Nacional José Martí. Servicio de Información. Bibliografía para el

temario del Congreso Cultural de La Habana. La Habana, 1967. 2v. (72-239500)

695. Knudsen, Jørgen. Økonomisk og politisk litteratur om udviklingslandene: annoteret bibliografi. With P. Neersø og F. N. Christensen. 3. udg. København, Mellemfolkeligt samvirke, 1969. 50p. (73-524832)

696. Malengreau, Guy. Théorie générale des institutions politiques des pays en développement; bibliographie sommaire. Avec la collaboration de A. Lecointre et J. Agreda. Louvain, Institut d'étude des pays en développement, 1967? 33 ℓ. (71-487726)

697. ReQua, Eloise G. The developing nations; a guide to information sources concerning their economic, political, technical, and social problems. With J. Statham. Foreword by G. I. Blankesten. Detroit, Gale Research Co., 1965. 339p. (65-17576)

698. Sørensen, Just. Teknisk udvikling i u-lande. Annoteret bibliografi. København K, Danmarks Tekniske Bibliotek, ø. Voldgade 10, 1969. 30 ℓ. (75-544959)

699. U. S. Information Agency. Nation building and economic modernization. Washington, U. S. Information Agency, Information Center Service, 1968. 71p. (70-602570)

UNITED NATIONS

700. American Association for the United Nations. Read your way to world understanding; a selected annotated reading guide of books about the United Nations and the world in which it works for peace and human welfare. New York, Scarecrow Press, 1963. 307p. (63-7454)

701. Brimmer, Brenda. A guide to the use of United Nations documents (including reference to the specialized agencies and special U.N. bodies). Dobbs Ferry, N.Y., Oceana Publications, 1962. 272p. (63-3667)

702. Fialová, Božena. Publikace Spojených národů v Universitní knihovně v Brně. Brno, Univ. knihovna, t. G 03, Vyškov, 1969. 91p. (71-522126)

703. McConaughy, John Bothwell. A student's guide to United Nations documents and their use. With H.J. Blanks. With a pref. by J. Groesbeck. New York, Council on International Relations and United Nations Affairs, 1969. 17p. (75-11872)
    A good guide to basic U.N. documents.

704. Syracuse University. Maxwell School of Citizenship and Public Affairs. An index to the publications of the United Nations, its affiliated agencies, and regional international organizations in the Syracuse University libraries... Syracuse, N.Y., 1963. 21 ℓ. (NUC65-55169)

705. Thompson, Elizabeth M. Resources for teaching about the United Nations, with annotated bibliography. Prepared for the Committee on International Relations. Washington, National Education Association of the United States, 1962. 90p. (62-20974)

706. United Nations. Dag Hammarskjold Library. Current issues; a selected bibliography on subjects of concern to the United Nations. no. 1- Dec. 1965- . New York, United Nations. no. in v. (74-23836)

707. United Nations. Economic Commission for Asia and the Far East. Check list of Economic Commission for Asia and the Far East documents. Bangkok, Thailand, 1959. 2v. (78-16676)

708. United Nations. Library. List of selected articles. no. 1- Sept. 20, 1949- . New York. no. (59-459)

709. _____. United Nations documents index. Jan. 1950- . Lake Success. v. (51-5008)

710. United Nations. Office of Public Information. United Nations publications. New York, 1945/48- . v. (50-1398rev2)

711. U.S. Office of Education. The United Nations and related organizations; a bibliography. Prepared in the International Educational Relations Branch. Washington, 1960. 17p. (HEW60-128)

U.S. CONGRESS

712. Andriot, Jeanne K. Checklist & index of congressional hearings, 85th Congress, 2d Session. With J.L. Andriot. Arlington, Va., Documents Index, 1958- . v. (58-59686)

713. Tompkins, Dorothy Louise (Campbell) Culver. Changes in Congress: proposals to change Congress, term of members of the House; a bibliography. Berkeley, Institute of Governmental Studies, University of California, 1966. 43p. (66-4247)

U.S. DEPT. OF STATE

714. U.S. Dept of State. Historical Office. Department of State publications on diplomatic history, international law, and the conduct of foreign relations. Washington, U.S. Govt. Print. Off., 1961. 17p. (SD62-1)

U.S.--DIPLOMATIC AND CONSULAR SERVICE

715. U.S. Civil Service Commission. Library. Managing overseas personnel. Washington, U.S. Govt. Print. Off., 1970. 86p. (78-610106)

U.S.--EXECUTIVE DEPARTMENTS--DIRECTORIES

716. Wynkoop, Sally. Directories of Government agencies. With D.W. Parish. Rochester, N.Y., Libraries Unlimited, 1969. 242p. (70-84652)

U.S.--FOREIGN OPINION, FRENCH

717. Faÿ, Bernard. Bibliographie critique des ouvrages français relatifs aux États-Unis (1770-1800). New York, B. Franklin, 1968. 108p. (68-56725)

U.S.--FOREIGN RELATIONS

718. African Bibliographic Center. U.S. treaties and agreements with countries in Africa, 1957 to mid-1963. Washington, 1965. 13p. (66-50749)

719. Bemis, Samuel Flagg. Guide to the diplomatic history of the United States, 1775-1921. With G.G. Griffin. (reprint) Washington, U.S. Govt. Print. Off., 1935; Gloucester, Mass., P. Smith, 1959. 979p. (35-26001)

720. Brown, J. Cudd. Administration of United States foreign affairs; a bibliography. With M.B. Rieg. University Park, Fred Lewis Pattee Library, Pennsylvania State University, 1968. 126 ℓ. (77-626408)
    A classified bibliography with good coverage.

721. Henthorn, William E. Korean views of America, 1954-64; an annotated bibliography. Honolulu, Research Translations, East-West Center, 1965. 66p. (71-5214)

722. Irick, Robert L. American-Chinese relations, 1784-1941; a survey of the Chinese-language materials at Harvard. Cambridge, Mass., Committee on American Far Eastern Policy Studies, Dept. of History, Harvard University; distributed by Harvard University Press, 1960. 269p. (60-4930)

723. Liu, Kwang-Ching. Americans and Chinese; a historical essay and a bibliography. Cambridge, Harvard University Press, 1963. 211p. (63-19141)

724. Plischke, Elmer. American diplomacy; a bibliography of bibliographies, and commentaries. College Park, Bureau of Governmental Research, College of Business and Public Administration, University of Maryland, 1957. 27p. (57-63088)

725. ―――. American foreign relations, a bibliography of official sources. College Park, Bureau of Governmental Research, College of Business and Public Administration, University of Maryland, 1956, c1955. 71p. (56-62681)

726. Steinicke, Dietrich. Quellenindex zur Cubakrise. Eine Zusammenstellung aller im Zusammenhang mit der Quarantäne Cubas im Jahre 1962 bekanntgewordenen Dokumente mit Inhaltsangaben sowie mit einem völkerrechtlichen Schlagwortverzeichnis zusammengestellt und bearb. unter Mitarbeit von Wolfdieter Harbeck. Hamburg, Frankfurt a. M. und Berlin, Metzner in Kommission, 1969. 400p. (70-414273)

727. Trask, David F. A bibliography of United States-Latin American relations since 1810; a selected list of eleven thousand published references. Comp. and ed. with Michael C. Meyer and Roger R. Trask. Lincoln, University of Nebraska Press, 1968. 441p. (67-14421)
    An excellent and very useful bibliography. Provides a good compilation of material, including works in French, German, Italian, Russian, and Japanese. Books, articles, pamphlets, documents, unpublished materials, and various finding aids are listed; some are annotated. The guide is well organized and easy to use. There is some cross-referencing of material, and a detailed index of authors.

728. U.S. Dept. of State. External Research Division. Foreign area and foreign policy research papers. Washington, 1960. 18p. (61-60572)

729. U.S. Dept. of State. Film Library. The United States and Western Europe; a 29 minute foreign policy briefing film analyzing the nature and development of U.S. policy toward Western Europe since the end of World War II. Produced by the U.S. Department of State. Washington, U.S. Govt. Print. Off., 1968. 7p. (76-600559)
    This is a Discussion guide, Dept. of State Publication no. 8123.

730. U.S. Information Service, Ottawa. Canadian-American relations, 1867-1967; a compilation of selected documents concerning the relations between Canada and the United States during the first century of Canada's Confederation. Ottawa, 1967. 3v. (72-413807)

U.S.--GOVERNMENT PUBLICATIONS

731. Andriot, John L. Guide to U.S. Government

serials & periodicals, 1969- . McLean,
Va., Documents Index. v. in (75-7027)
   Basic volumes published in March and a
   supplement, which up dates the information through June 30 of each year, issued
   in September.

732. Childs, James Bennett. Government document
   bibliography in the United States and elsewhere. 3d ed. Washington, U. S. Govt.
   Print. Off., 1942. 78p. (42-38637)
      Includes materials on the Confederate
      States of America, and the League of Na-
      tions.

733. Government reference books. 1st-   ed.;
   1968-69- . Littleton, Colo., Libraries Unlimited. v. (76-146307)

734. Mechanic, Sylvia. Annotated list of selected
   United States Government publications avail-
   able to depository libraries. Compiled for
   the University of the State of New York, the
   New York State Library. New York, H. W.
   Wilson Co., 1971. 407p. (78-99430)

735. Navon, Anita. Research materials for Slavists:
   U. S. Government sources. Washington,
   Slavic Bibliographic and Documentation Center, Association of Research Libraries, 1970.
   22 ℓ. (71-23870)

736. New York (State). State Library, Albany. Legislative Reference Library. Current checklists of State publications. Albany, 1967.
   5 ℓ. (70-261673)

737. Selected United States Government publications.
   1968- . McLean, Va., Documents Index.
   v. (73-18389)
      Covers all types of U. S. Government pub-
      lications.

738. U.S. Congress. House. Committee on Banking and Currency. List of publications issued by Committee on Banking and Currency: hearings, reports, and committee prints, 39th-91st Congresses (1865-1970). 91st Congress, 2d session. Washington, U.S. Govt. Print. Off., 1970. 151p. (71-610927)

739. U.S. Library of Congress. Exchange and Gift Division. Monthly checklist of State publications. v. 1- Jan. 1910- . Washington, U.S. Govt. Print. Off. v. (10-8924rev3)

740. _____. Non-GPO imprints received in the Library of Congress, July 1967 through December 1969; a selective checklist. Washington, Library of Congress, 1970. 73p. (70-606580)

741. U.S. Library of Congress. Serial Division. Popular names of U.S. Government reports; a catalog. Rev. and enl. Compiled by Bernard A. Bernier, Jr. and Charlotte M. David. Washington, Library of Congress; U.S. Govt. Print. Off., 1970. 43p. (77-608261)

742. U.S. Superintendent of Documents. Catalog of the public documents of Congress and all departments of the government of the United States for the period Mar. 4, 1893-Dec. 31, 1940. Washington, U.S. Govt. Print. Off., 1896-1945. 25v. (6-12151)

743. _____. Checklist of United State public documents, 1789-1909. 3d ed. Washington, U.S. Govt. Print. Off., 1911. 1707p. (12-35731)

744. _____. Monthly catalog of United States Government publications. Washington, U.S. Govt. Print. Off., 1895- . v. (4-18088)

745. _____. Tables of and annotated index to the

congressional series of United States public documents. Washington, U.S. Govt. Print. Off., 1902. 769p. (2-13262)

746. University of Illinois at Chicago Circle. Library. A guide to selected United States Government publications in the Library, University of Illinois at Chicago Circle. For students of history and political science. Compiled by Y. Nakata, documents librarian. Chicago, 1970. 59p. (70-630423)
 A brief guide to the more important U.S. Govt. publications.

747. Wilcox, Jerome Kear. Official defense publications; guide to state and federal publications. Berkeley, Bureau of Public Administration, University of California, 1941-45. 9v. (41-46006rev4)

U.S.--HISTORY--CIVIL WAR

748. Bartlett, John Russell. The literature of the rebellion; a catalogue of books and pamphlets relating to the Civil War in the United States, and on subjects growing out of that event, together with works on American slavery, and essays from reviews on the same subjects. Westport, Conn., Negro Universities Press, 1970. 477p. (77-109311)

U.S.--HISTORY--REVOLUTION--CAUSES

749. Adams, Thomas Randolph. American independence: the growth of an idea; a bibliographical study of the American political pamphlets printed between 1764 and 1776 dealing with the dispute between Great Britain and her colonies. Providence, Brown University Press, 1965. 200p. (62-16995)

Lists works dealing with the causes of the U.S. revolution.

U.S.--HISTORY--REVOLUTION--SOURCES

750. U.S. Library of Congress. Manuscript Division. <u>Calendar of the correspondence of George Washington, Commander in Chief of the Continental Army with the Continental Congress. Prepared from the original manuscripts in the Library of Congress</u> by J.C. Fitzpatrick, Division of Manuscripts. New York, B. Franklin, 1970. 741p. (72-124310)

U.S.--POLITICS

751. Jonas, Frank H. <u>Bibliography on Western politics; selected, annotated, with introductory essays.</u> Salt Lake City, Institute of Government, University of Utah, 1958. 167p. (NUC58-62)

U.S.--POLITICS AND GOVERNMENT

752. Connery, Robert Howe. <u>Reading guide in politics and government.</u> With R.H. Leach and J. Zikmund II. Washington, National Council for the Social Studies, 1966. 85p. (66-26280)

753. No entry under this number

754. Gaines, Pierce Welch. <u>Political works on concealed authorship in the United States, 1789-1810, with attributions.</u> Rev. and enl. ed. Hamden, Conn., Shoe String Press, 1965. 190p. (65-17720)

755. _____. <u>Political writings in the young Republic...</u> (In American Antiquarian Society,

Worcester, Mass. Proceedings. Worcester.
v. 76, pt. 2(1967) p. 261-292) (A67-317)

756. Kansas Free Press. Current bibliography and
abridged directory of the American right-wing.
2d ed. Lawrence, Kansas, 1965. 15 ℓ.
(NUC69-26963)

757. Michigan. State University, East Lansing. Institute for Community Development and Services. Bibliography series. no. 1-   East
Lansing?, 1962- .   no. in   v.   (64-
64761)
Title varies: Bibliographic series.

758. Muller, Robert H. From radical left to extreme
right; a bibliography of current periodicals of
protest, controversy, advocacy, or dissent.
2d ed. rev. and enl. With T.J. Spahn, and
J.M. Spahn. Ann Arbor, Campus Publishers,
c1970- .   v.   (79-126558)

759. Tompkins, Dorothy Louise (Campbell) Culver.
Materials for the study of Federal Government. Chicago, Public Administration Service, 1948. 328p. (48-11485)

760. U.S. Congress. Senate. Committee on Government Operations. Organizing for national
security; a bibliography. Washington, U.S.
Govt. Print. Off., 1959. 77p.

U.S.--RURAL CONDITIONS

761. Payne, Raymond. The community; a classified,
annotated bibliography. With W.C. Bailey.
Athens, Dept. of Sociology and Anthropology,
University of Georgia, 1967. 142 ℓ. (68-
63535)

U.S. --SOCIAL CONDITIONS

762. Meyer, Jon K. Bibliography on the urban crisis; the behavioral, psychological, and sociological aspects of the urban crisis. Chevy Chase, Md., National Institute of Mental Health; for sale by the Supt. of Docs., U.S. Govt. Print. Off., Washington, 1969. 452p. (73-605766)
> Includes works on the race question in the U.S. and violence in the U.S.

U.S. --SUPREME COURT

763. Mersky, Roy M., comp. A selected bibliography on the history of the United States Supreme Court. n.p., 1969. 31 ℓ. (NUC70-6119)
> "Prepared for the Law and Political Science Sub-section of the American Library Association. Panel Discussion on 'Literature of the United States,' June 25, 1969."

764. Tompkins, Dorothy Louise (Campbell) Culver. The Supreme Court of the United States: a bibliography. Berkeley, Bureau of Public Administration, University of California, 1959. 217p. (60-62972)

URBAN RENEWAL--U.S.

765. U.S. Dept. of Housing and Urban Development. Library. Citizen and business participation in urban affairs; a bibliography. Washington, U.S. Govt. Print. Off., 1970. 84p. (72-607157)
> Includes works on volunteer workers in social service, the social aspects of industry and community organization.

766. ──────. Neighborhood conservation & property rehabilitation; a bibliography. Washington,

U.S. Govt. Print. Off., 1969. 78p. (79-605265)

URBANIZATION--AFRICA, WEST

767. Simms, Ruth P. Urbanization in West Africa, a review of current literature. Evanston, Ill., Northwestern University Press, 1965. 109p. (65-19464)

VENEZUELA--POLITICS AND GOVERNMENT

768. Zimmermann, Bruno. Neuere Studien 1945 bis 1968. Venezuela, Bielefeld Bertelsmann-Universitätsverlag, 1968. 91p. (72-488620) Also includes materials on the economic and social conditions in Venezuela.

VIETNAM--HISTORY

769. Jumper, Roy. Bibliography on the political and administrative history of Vietnam, 1802-1962, selected and annotated. Research assistants: Tran Nguyen Bong and Nguyen Thi Thu-Nga. Editor: Evelyn B. Gottlieb. Saigon?, Michigan State University, Vietnam Advisory Group, 1962. 179 ℓ. (SA62-1215)

VIETNAM (DEMOCRATIC REPUBLIC, 1946-   )

770. Kyriak, Theodore E. North Vietnam, 1957-1961; a bibliography and guide to contents of a collection of United States Joint Publications Research Service translations on microfilm. Annapolis, Research & Microfilm Publications, 196-? 62p. on 34 ℓ. (66-1212)

VIETNAMESE CONFLICT, 1961-

771. Legler, A. Der Krieg in Vietnam; Bericht und Bibliographie bis 30. 9. 1968. Mit K. Hubinek. Frankfurt am Main, Bernard & Graefe, 1969. 384p. (74-471087)

WAR

772. Everts, Philip P. Boeken over oorlog en vrede. Protestantse Stichting tot bevordering van het bibliotheekwezen en de lectuurvoorlichting in Nederland. Utrecht, Voorburg, 1968. 20p. (78-407666)

773. The two world wars; selective bibliography. Oxford, New York, Pergamon Press, 1965, c1964. 246p. (65-6499)

WATER--LAWS AND LEGISLATION--U. S.

774. Jacobstein, J. Myron. Water law bibliography, 1847-1965; source book on U.S. water and irrigation studies: legal, economic and political. With Roy M. Mersky. Silver Spring, MD., Jefferson Law Book Co., 1966. 249p. _____. _____; supplement no. 1- 1966/67- . v. (66-25234)

WEST INDIES--POLITICS

775. Institute of Jamaica, Kingston. West India Reference Library. A list of books on West Indian federation. 2d ed. by Anne Benewick. Kingston, Jamaica, 1962. 47p. (73-15482) Covers West Indian politics.

WHITE RUSSIA

776. Vakar, Nicholas P. A bibliographical guide to

Belorussia. Cambridge, Harvard University
Press, 1956. 63p. (54-11736)
Classified, with author index.

WISCONSIN

777. Wisconsin. University Bureau of Government.
A research inventory for Wisconsin. June
1959- . Madison. v. (61-62913)

WORLD POLITICS

778. European and Atlantic affairs. London, National
Book League with the European-Atlantic Movement, 1968. 24p. (77-362747)

779. Foreign Relations Library. Catalog of the Foreign Relations Library. Boston, G.K. Hall,
1969. 9v. (75-6133)
A fine resource tool for scholarly research.

780. Informations bibliographiques et documentaires en
science politique. Montréal, Centre de documentation et de recherches politiques. no.
in v. (79-10064)

781. International politics; a selective bibliography.
v.1- Mar. 1956- . Washington. v. in
(59-30881)

782. Kenworthy, Leonard Stout. Free and inexpensive
materials on world affairs. With R.A. Birdie.
3d ed. New York, Teachers College Press,
Columbia University, 1968, c1969. 65p.
(68-56447)

783. ———. Studying the world; selected resources.
2d ed. New York, Bureau of Publications,
Teachers College, Columbia University, 1965.
71p. (65-19212)

784. Kuhn, Jean. An annotated bibliography of selected unclassified materials published during 1966 on problems of development and internal defense. Washington, Foreign Service Institute, 1967. 113p. (79-16660)
Covers items on world politics and economic development.

785. Kyriak, Theodore E. International developments: a bibliography. no. 1- July/Sept. 1962- . Annapolis, Research Microfilms. v. (62-20265)
"Guide to contents of a collection of United States Joint Publications Research Service translations in the social sciences emanating from Africa, Latin America, Near East and Western Europe."

786. Meherally, Yusuf. The modern world, a political study syllabus. Bombay, Padma Publications ltd., 1945. 184p. (47-1545)

787. Savord, Ruth. World affairs; a foreign service reading list. With D. Wasson. Washington, Foreign Service Journal, 1954. 23p. (55-42653)

788. The United States and Europe; a bibliographical examination of thought expressed in American publications. Washington, Library of Congress, Reference Dept., European Affairs Division, 1948- v. (49-45626)

789. World Affairs Book Fair, 3d, 1956. Third world affairs book fair, political and cultural, 1956. Catalogue of the combined book exhibit. New York, Carnegie Endowment International Center, 1956. 31p.

YEMEN--POLITICS

790. U.S. Dept. of State. External Research Staff.

The tribes of Yemen; a list of Western language books and periodical articles containing information on the tribes of Yemen. Washington, 1964. 9p. (64-61257)

AUTHOR INDEX

Abernethy, George L., 442.
Adam, Melchior, 473.
Adams, Cynthia, 178.
Adams, Thomas R., 749.
Adler, Catherine E. M., 601.
African Bibliographic Center, 2, 718.
Akademie der Wissenschaften, Berlin. Institut für Wirtschaftswissenschaften. Bibliothek, 690.
Alaska. State Library, Juneau, 181.
Alderfer, Harold F., 7.
Alexandrowicz, Charles H., 311.
Altbach, Philip G., 83.
American Association for the United Nations, 700.
American Association of Law Libraries. Committee on Foreign and International Law, 316.
American Bar Foundation, 328.
American Bar Foundation. Cromwell Library, 12, 13, 329.
American Bar Foundation. Project on Unauthorized Practice of the Law, 330.
American behavioral scientist, 602.
American Law Student Association. Techno-legal Committee, 218.
American Universities Field Staff, 82.
American University, Washington, D. C. Special Operations Research Office, 395.
Andrews, Joseph L., 331.
Andriot, Jeanne K., 360, 712.
Andriot, John L., 731
Argentine Republic. Congreso. Biblioteca. Referencia General, 102.
Association for Education in Citizenship, 603.
Association of American Law Schools, 269.
Aufricht, Hans, 232, 233, 352.
Augustus M. Kelley (Firm), 604.

Azim, M., 105.
Aziz, Khursheed K., 212.

Bachelder, Glen L., 161.
Baker, George H., 475.
Baksh, S., 164.
Barnes, Harry E., 605.
Barros, Maria N. M. M. de, 606.
Bartlett, John R., 748.
Bates, Frederick L., 446.
Bayitch, S. A., 666.
Beale, Joseph H., 304.
Beardsley, Arthur S., 317, 333, 334, 335, 336, 337, 348, 416.
Beck, Carl, 142.
Becker, Fritz, 396.
Beeley, Brian W., 688.
Beittel, William, 479.
Belgium. Ministère des finances. Bibliothèque centrale, 648.
Belgium. Parlement. Bibliothèque, 292.
Bemis, Samuel F., 719.
Berlin. Stadtbibliothek, 175.
Besterman, Theodore, 33.
Bhatia, Mohan, 52.
Bigelow, Robert P., 219.
Bitz, Ira, 681.
Bodde, Derk, 294.
Boehm, Eric H., 37, 608.
Böhmer, Georg W., 122.
Bonn. Archiv für Gesamtdeutsche Fragen, 177.
Booth, David A., 413.
Borg, Dorothy, 132.
Boston Public Library, 609.
Boston University. African Studies Program, 540, 541.
Boston University. Area Development Center, 573.
Boston University. Bureau of Public Administration, 669.
Boston University. Libraries, 6.
Bowker, Richard R., 480.
Bozza, Tommaso, 481.
Bradley, Phillips, 406.
Branch, Melville C., 68.

Branning, Rosalind L., 455.
Breuer, Ernest H., 201.
Breycha-Vanthier, Arthur C. von, 353.
Brimmer, Brenda, 701.
Brindley, Mary E., 482.
British Library of Political and Economic Science. London, 483, 484.
Brittain, Robert P., 387.
Brock, Clifton, 485, 486.
Brode, John, 594.
Brodowski, Joyce H., 258.
Brookings Institution, Washington, D.C., 487.
Brooks, Alexander D., 78.
Brooks, Robert C., 407.
Brown, J. Cudd, 720.
Brown, Lyle C., 267.
Budapest. Magyar Közgazdaságtudományi Egyetem, 611.
Buell, Raymond L., 136.
Burchfield, Laverne, 488.
Bureau of Social Science Research, Washington, D.C., 567.
Burnham, Walter D., 141.
Bussmann, Christian, 300.

Caldwell, Lynton K., 590.
California. Legislature. Assembly. Legislative Reference Service, 49.
California. State College, San Diego. Library, 155.
California. University. Institute of Governmental Studies, 118, 119, 120, 121, 675.
California. University. University at Los Angeles. Center of Latin American Studies, 98.
Cam, Helen M., 185.
Camurani, Ercole, 364.
Canadian Council for International Co-operation, 691.
Carlson, Andrew R., 171.
Carnegie Endowment for International Peace, 238.
Carnell, Francis, 674.
Carpenter, Glenn B., 350.
Carter, April, 448.
Cervin, Ulf, 327.
Chambliss, William J., 659.
Charlot, Jean, 459.

Chilcote, Ronald H., 259, 419.
Childs, Harwood L., 568.
Childs, James B., 732.
Clarke, Jack A., 612.
Clemens, Walter C., 588.
Cohn, Bernard S., 213.
Coke, Sir Edward, 271.
Colchester, Eng. University of Essex. Library, 186.
Cole, Allan B., 96.
Collart, Yves, 129.
Collotti Pischel, Enrica, 86.
Colorado. University. Bureau of Governmental Research and Service, 87.
Columbia University. Faculty of Political Science, 489.
Conference on North Atlantic Community, Bruges, 1957, 428.
Connecticut. Office of State Planning, 574.
Connery, Robert H., 752.
Coolidge, John E., 187.
Corbin, Doris, 613.
Cordier, Henri, 21, 53.
Cornell University. Graduate School of Business and Public Administration, 542, 543.
Cornog, Geoffrey Y., 525, 566.
Cosgrove, Carol A., 156.
Court of Justice of the European Communities, 114.
Cowley, John D., 305.
Crown, James T., 252.
Cumming, Sir John G., 115.
Currier, Thomas F., 205.

Dahl, Richard C., 249.
Decalo, Samuel, 677.
DeGrazia, Alfred, 545.
Delaney, Robert F., 100.
Denmark. Arbejds-, familie- og socialministeriernes bibliotek, 546.
Dennis, Jack S., 526.
Desrochers, Edmond, 614.
Deutsch, Karl W., 417.
Deutsches Institut für Zeitgeschichte. Bibliothek, 32.
Dias, Reginald W. M., 251.

Dolléans, Édouard, 652.
Dortmund. Stadtbücherei, 381.
Douma, J., 193.
Dramard, Eugène, 301.
Duke, Richard D., 69.
Dutschke, Rudi, 91.

Eaton, Andrew J., 490.
Egbert, Donald D., 653.
Engová, Helena, 125.
Essen, Jan L. F. van, 128.
Everts, Philip P., 772.

Faber, Karl G., 174.
Fairbank, John K., 54.
Fatemi, Ali M. S., 421.
Faÿ, Bernard, 717.
Fialová, Božena, 702.
Finland. Valtion painatuskeskus, 165.
Finlayson, Jennifer A. S., 26.
Flood, Kenneth U., 683.
Foreign Relations Library, 779.
Francisco, Vicente J., 272.
Freedom Institute, Iowa Wesleyan College, 682.
Frey, Frederick W., 693.
Friedman, Robert S., 383.
Fritschler, A. L., 70.

Gaines, Pierce W., 754, 755.
Gáliczky, Eva, 97.
Galloway, George B., 491.
Gard, Richard A., 492.
Gardin, Natacha, 615.
Gardner, Charles S., 55.
Garling, Anthea, 35.
Garrison, Lloyd W., 462.
Gautam, Brijendra P., 524.
Geiger, H. Kent, 138, 595.
Germany (Federal Republic, 1949-   ). Bundesministerium für Wirtschaft. Bibliothek, 616.
Gibson, Frank K., 447.
Gierth, Sieglinde, 260.
Ginsburg, Ruth B., 325.

Glenn, Norval D., 596.
Goldwater, Walter, 654.
Goodey, Brian R., 140.
Goodwin, George, 386.
Government Affairs Foundation, 411.
Grandin, A., 302.
Graves, William B., 670.
Gray, Charles H., 450.
Gray, Richard A., 41.
Gt. Brit. Central Office of Information Reference Division, 188.
Gt. Brit. Foreign Office, 62.
Gt. Brit. Ministry of Overseas Development. Library, 137.
Gt. Brit. Public Record Office, 189, 195, 196, 197, 198, 199.
Gt. Brit. Stationery Office, 190.
Greer, Sarah, 79.
Grisoli, Angelo, 314.
Gropp, Arthur E., 38.
Gross, Charles, 409.
Groth, Alexander, 579.
Grotius Society, London, Library, 225.
Gumpert, Ute, 150.
Gunzenhäuser, Max, 445.
Gutkind, Peter C. W., 3.
Guttenberg, Albert Z., 71.

Hague. International Court of Justice, 194.
Hague. Palace of Peace. Library, 451, 452.
Halász, D., 368.
Halasz de Beky, I. L., 210.
Hale, Barbara M., 617.
Halévy, Balfour J., 111.
Hamburg. Europa-Kolleg, 157.
Hamilton, F. E. I., 575.
Hanna, Paul R., 618.
Hargrett, Lester, 214.
Harmon, Robert B., 493, 494, 495, 496, 497.
Harrison, James D., 72.
Harvard University. East Asian Research Center, 63.
Harvard University International Program in Taxation, 678.

Harvard University. Law School. Library, 226, 273, 274, 275, 532, 685.
Harvard University. Library, 22, 521.
Haupt, Georges, 221.
Havana. Biblioteca Nacional José Martí. Servicio de Información, 694.
Hawaii. Dept. of Planning and Economic Development, 202.
Heimer, Franz-Wilhelm, 44.
Heinz, Grete, 166.
Heitman, Sidney, 46.
Henthorn, William E., 721.
Herndon, James, 671.
Hertefelt, Marcel d', 11.
Hewitt, William H., 570.
Hicks, Frederick C., 276.
Higham, Robin, 399.
Hill, William S., 206.
Historical Association, London, 498.
Hoffman, Bernard G., 619.
Holland, Henry M., 499.
Holmes, Joan C., 27.
Horecky, Paul L., 29, 147, 582.
Horne, Norman P., 23.
Horrocks, Sidney, 356.
Hoselitz, Berthold F., 620.
Howell, Margaret A., 277.
Hucker, Charles O., 56.
Hunt, Robert N.C., 92.

India (Republic). Government of India Publication Branch, 211.
Indian Institute of Public Administration, 180.
Indiana. University. Library. Government Publications Dept., 528.
Indonesia. Department Penerangan, 217.
Information Research Associates, 220.
Institute for Rural America, 529.
Institute of Jamaica, Kingston. West India Reference Library, 775.
Institute of Public Administration, New York, 547, 548.
Interamerican Children's Institute. Library, 621.
International Association of Legal Science, 278.

International Committee for Social Sciences Documentation, 36, 622.
International Labor Office. Central Library and Documentation Branch, 597.
Irick, Robert L., 722.
Irion, Frederick C., 425.
Istituto per la scienza dell'amministrazione pubblica, 372.

Jacobstein, J. Myron, 279, 338, 339, 774.
Jäger, Eckhard, 172.
al-Jam'īyah al-Misrīyah lil-Qānūn al-Duwalī. al-Maktabah, 227.
Japan. Mombushō. Daigaku Gakujutsu-kyoku, 315.
Jiang, Joseph, 66.
Johnson, Charles W., 391.
Johnson, Harold S., 236.
Jonas, Frank H., 751.
Jones, Charles O., 463.
Jumper, Roy, 769.
Juris, Gail, 144.

Kansas Free Press, 756.
Kantor, Harry, 460.
Kasfir, Nelson, 8.
Keitt, Lawrence, 340.
Kenworthy, Leonard S., 782, 783.
Kenyon, Carleton W., 45, 355.
Knudsen, Jørgen, 695.
Koers, Albert W., 380.
Kronenberg, Henry H., 623.
Kuhn, Jean, 784.
Kyriak, Theodore E., 18, 57, 64, 93, 94, 148, 216, 254, 583, 624, 770, 785.

Labour Party (Gt. Brit.), 257.
Lancaster, Lucy L., 502.
Landheer, Bartholomeus, 228, 572.
Larrea Holguín, Juan I., 297.
Lasswell, Harold D., 537.
Leamer, Laurence E., 625.
Legler, A., 771.
Leipzig. Stadt- und Bezirksbibliothek, 176.

Leipziger Kommissions- und Grossbuchhandel, 626.
Leister, D.R., 50.
Leuthold, David A., 51.
Levine, Robert A., 503.
Lewis, Peter R., 627.
Lian-The, 24.
Liboiron, Albert A., 162.
Liège. Université. Institut de sociologie, 549, 550, 551.
Ligthart Schenk, A.H., 657.
Lincoln's Inn, London. Library, 280.
Lindsay, Robert O., 167.
Lipen, Martin, 281.
Liu, Kwang-Ching, 723.
Livingston, David T., 389.
Livneh, Ernst, 312, 313.
London. University. Institute of Advanced Legal Studies, 295, 299, 318, 341.
London. University. Restatement of African Law Project, 291.
London. University. University College. Library, 31.
Lopez, Manuel D., 651.
Lorenz, Robert, 73.
Los Angeles. Public Library. Municipal Reference Library, 408.
Los Angeles. University of Southern California. Library, 401.
Loventhal, Milton, 584.
Lozzi, Carlo, 410.

McCarthy, Betty A., 580.
McConaughy, John B., 703.
McCoy, Ralph E., 366.
McCulloch, John R., 504.
Macdonald, Hugh, 204.
Macdonald, Hugn I., 151.
McDougall, Donald, 505.
McGehee, A.L., 351.
McGill University, Montreal. French Canada Studies Programme, 458.
McGill University, Montreal. French Canada Studies Programme. Bibliothèque, 261.

Maier, Hans, 506.
Malengreau, Guy, 696.
Malwad, N. M., 76.
Manchester Incorporated Law Library Society, 307.
Mao, Tsê-tung, 379.
Marke, Julius J., 89, 342.
Marquis, Stewart D., 437.
Mars, David, 552.
Maryland. Morgan State College, Baltimore. Urban Studies Institute, 30.
Maryland. University. Bureau of Governmental Research, 507.
Mason, John B., 630.
Mason, Lois E., 262.
Matczak, Sebastian A., 508.
Mattei, Rodolfo de, 509.
Matthews, Daniel G., 146.
Maybury, Catherine M., 433.
Mechanic, Sylvia, 734.
Medsker, Karen, 159.
Meherally, Yusuf, 786.
Menge, Paul E., 662.
Mersky, Roy M., 343, 763.
Mesa, Rosa Q., 43, 84, 390.
Meshenberg, Michael J., 145.
Messler Library, 373.
Meyer, Jon K., 762.
Meyriat, Jean, 510.
Michigan. State Library, Lansing, 456.
Michigan. State University, East Lansing. Institute for Community Development and Services, 357, 392, 757.
Michigan. University. Bureau of Industrial Relations, 553.
Michigan. University. Institute of Public Administration, 554.
Michigan. University. William L. Clements Library, 344.
Mickey, Margaret P., 58.
Middle East Institute, Washington, D. C., 422.
Mid-European Law Project, 296, 298, 310, 324, 349.
Miley, Arthur L., 555.
Mill, John S., 400.

Miller, William R., 441.
Minnesota. University. Public Administration Center, 576.
Mississippi. University. Bureau of Governmental Research, 404.
Mohl, Robert von, 511.
Mote, Frederick W., 59.
Mowlana, Hamid, 384.
Mulhauser, Roland A., 369.
Muller, Robert H., 758.
Munro, William B., 412.
Murray, D.J., 427.

National Association of State Libraries. Public Document Clearing House Committee, 358.
National Book League, London, 90, 108.
National Municipal League, 112.
National Opinion Research Center, 650.
National Science Library, 591.
Naude, Gabriel, 512.
Navon, Anita, 735.
Needham, Christopher D., 631.
Netherlands (Kingdom, 1815-). Centraal bureau voor de Statistiek, 632.
Nettlau, Max, 14.
New Jersey. Dept. of Community Affairs, 424.
New Jersey. State College, Trenton. Roscoe L. West Library, 4, 19.
New York Public Library, 464.
New York State Library, Albany, 635.
New York State Library, Albany. Legislative Reference Library, 110, 556, 736.
New York University. School of Law. Library, 282.
Niaz, Mohammad A., 443, 557.
Nick, William V., 388.
North American Congress on Latin America, 600.
North Atlantic Treaty Organization, 429, 430, 431.
Notz, Rebecca L. L., 345.

Ohio. State Library, Columbus, 436.
Oko, Adolph S., 668.
Ola, Israel O., 370.
Olivart, Ramón de Dalmau y de Olivart, marqués de, 240.

Oppenheim, Leonard, 283.
Ordine avvocati e procuratori di Milano. Biblioteca, 284.
Organization for European Economic Cooperation, 158, 438.
Otto, Frieda, 42.
Ozols, Selma A., 268.

Paisley, William J., 598.
Paklons, L. L., 160.
Palotai, Olga C., 434.
Pålsson, Lennart, 285.
Pan American Union. Columbus Memorial Library, 439, 453, 667.
Park, Hong-Kyu, 255.
Parker, Ted F., 374.
Parrish, Michael, 586.
Paulsen, David F., 109.
Payne, Raymond, 761.
Pegnetter, Richard, 143.
Pelikán, Bohumil, 362.
Pemberton, John E., 191.
Peritz, Rene, 377.
Perticone, Giacomo, 323.
Pickus, Robert, 454.
Pimsleur, Meira G., 346.
Pindić, Dimitrije, 229.
Pinson, Koppel S., 418.
Plischke, Elmer, 724, 725.
Plucknett, Theodore F. T., 286.
Pogány, András H., 513.
Press, Charles, 393, 672.
Princeton University, Library, 514.
Public Administration Service, 414.
Public Administration Service. Public Automated Systems Service, 558.
Public Affairs Information Service, 636.
Public Affairs Research Council of Louisiana, inc., 375, 376.
Public Personnel Association, 559.
Puget, Henry, 1.
Pullen, William R., 359.
Pundeff, Marin V., 47.

Quebec (Province). Dept. of Natural Resources. Library, 420.
Quezon, Philippines. University of the Philippines. Library, 287.

Rachavan, Susheila, 527.
Rahman, M.A., 444.
Rajasthan, India. High Court of Judicature. Library, 288.
ReQua, Eloise G., 697.
Riascos Sánchez, Blanca, 397.
Riddleberger, Peter B., 17.
Riesser, Hans E., 173.
Robinson, Jacob, 230.
Rodgers, Frank, 200.
Roeckelein, Jon E., 593.
Rogers, William C., 237.
Rokkan, Stein, 569.
Roper, D., 250.
Ross, Joel E., 378.
Royal Institute of Public Administration, 192.
Rubel, Maximilien, 382.
Ruffmann, Karl H., 95.

Sable, Martin H., 67, 263.
Samford, Clarence D., 637.
Savord, Ruth, 787.
Schautz, Jane, 515.
Schroeder, Theodore A., 365.
Schwab, Moïse, 16.
Seckler-Hudson, Catheryn, 561.
Seidman, Joel I., 101.
Selim, George D., 15.
Senn, Peter R., 638.
Setaro, Franklyn C., 533.
Sewell, John, 367.
Shiner, Patricia, 103.
Shulman, Frank J., 248.
Shurter, Edwin D., 516.
Silva, Ruth C., 139.
Simms, Ruth P., 767.
Singapore (City). National Library, 104.
Sipkov, Ivan, 293.

Skarprud, Elsa, 435.
Skive kommunebibliotek, 371.
Slavens, Thomas P., 639.
Smith, Chitra M., 538.
Social Science Research Council. Committee on Survey of Research on Crime and Criminal Justice, 116.
Socialist Labor Party, 658.
Sørensen, Just, 698.
Sørensen, Per, 127.
South Dakota. State Legislative Research Council, 663, 664.
Special Libraries Association. Social Science Group, 562.
Speeckaert, Georges P., 222, 223.
Spell, Lota May H., 264.
Spitz, Allan A., 563.
Stammhammer, Josef, 642, 656.
Steinicke, Dietrich, 726.
Stover, John F., 684.
Sumner, William G., 643.
Suzuki, Peter T., 689.
Sweet and Maxwell, ltd., London, 308.
Sydney. University. Law School. Library, 289.
Syracuse University. Maxwell School of Citizenship and Public Affairs, 704.
Szekely, Kalman S., 534.
Szladits, Charles, 107, 303.

Tamkoc, Metin, 687.
Tamuno, Olufunmilayo G., 154.
Tarozzi, Ermanno, 577.
Television Information Office, New York. Library, 679.
Tennessee. State Library and Archives, Nashville. Archives Section, 113.
Terauchi, Mildred, 203.
Texas. University. Institute of Public Affairs, 680.
Texas. University. School of Law, 326.
Thompson, Elizabeth M., 705.
Thompson, Olive, 644.
Todd, William B., 48.
Tompkins, Dorothy L.C.C., 28, 88, 123, 415, 530, 535, 673, 713, 759, 764.

Trask, David F., 727.
Tsien, Tsuen-hsuin, 134.
Turano, Peter J., 394.
Turnbull, Augustus B., 170.

Uchida, Naosaku, 60.
United Kingdom National Committee of Comparative Law, 309.
United Nations. Dag Hammarskjold Library, 182, 706.
United Nations. Economic Commission for Asia and the Far East, 707.
United Nations. Library, 708, 709.
United Nations. Office of Legal Affairs, 686.
United Nations. Office of Public Information, 710.
United Nations. Secretariat, 10.
United Nations. Technical Assistance Administration, 564.
United Nations Educational, Scientific and Cultural Organization, 645.
U.S. Air Force Academy. Library, 74.
U.S. Civil Service Commission, 80, 81.
U.S. Civil Service Commission. Library. 457, 715.
U.S. Commission on Intergovernmental Relations, 163.
U.S. Congress. House. Committee on Banking and Currency, 738.
U.S. Congress. Senate. Committee on Government Operations, 760.
U.S. Congress. Senate. Library, 361.
U.S. Dept. of Housing and Urban Development, 75.
U.S. Dept. of Housing and Urban Development. Library, 208, 765, 766.
U.S. Dept. of State. External Research Division, 135, 728.
U.S. Dept. of State. External Research Staff, 169, 539, 646, 790.
U.S. Dept. of State. Film Library, 729.
U.S. Dept. of State. Historical Office, 714.
U.S. Dept. of State. Library Division, 423.
U.S. Dept. of the Army, 65, 149, 265, 432, 585.
U.S. Dept. of the Army. Army Library, 587.
U.S. Dept. of the Interior. Library, 215, 347.
U.S. Federal Aviation Administration. Library Services Division, 130.

U.S. Information Agency, 241, 699.
U.S. Information Service, Ottawa, 730.
U.S. Library of Congress. Division of Bibliography, 106, 465, 466, 467, 468, 469, 470.
U.S. Library of Congress. Exchange and Gift Division, 739, 740.
U.S. Library of Congress. General Reference and Bibliography Division, 9, 242, 426, 536, 660.
U.S. Library of Congress. Law Library, 39, 40.
U.S. Library of Congress. Legislative Reference Service, 184, 592.
U.S. Library of Congress. Manuscript Division, 168, 750.
U.S. Library of Congress. Serial Division, 741.
U.S. National Clearinghouse for Mental Health Information, 581.
U.S. Office of Education, 711.
U.S. Social Security Administration. Office of Research and Statistics, 531.
U.S. Special Staff for Labor Relations and Equal Opportunity, 402.
U.S. Superintendent of Documents, 742, 743, 744, 745.
U.S. Veterans Administration. Medical and General Reference Library, 565.
United World Federalists, 243.
Universal Reference System, 517.
University of Illinois at Chicago Circle, Library, 746.
Utah. State Board of Education, 403.

Vakar, Nicholas P., 776.
Vandiver, Richard, 117.
Varley, Douglas H., 245.
Venys, Ladislav, 5.
Virginia. State Library, Richmond, 518.
Völgyes, Iván, 209.

Wallmén, Olof, 676.
Ward, Robert E., 247.
Washington University, St. Louis, Libraries, 519.
Wasserman, Paul, 126.
Weaver, Jerry L., 266.
Webster, John B., 253.

Wheeler, Lora J., 461.
Whitmore, William H., 385.
Wiarda, Howard J., 131.
Wilcox, Jerome K., 183, 747.
Willot, Paul, 589.
Wisconsin. University. Bureau of Government, 777.
Wisconsin. University. Dept. of Political Science, 520.
Witherell, Julian W., 179.
Woolley, Harry C., 207.
World Affairs Book Fair, 3d, 1956, 789.
World Peace Foundation, Boston, 354.
Wu, Wen-chin, 61.
Wynar, Lubomyr R., 471, 522, 647.
Wynkoop, Sally, 716.

Yunesuko Higashi Ajia Bunka Kenkyū Sentā, Tokyo, 20.

Zawadzki, Stanislaw M., 578.
Zawodny, Janusz K., 244.
Zentralbibliothek der Bundeswehr, 398.
Ziervogel, Barbara, 85.
Zile, Zigurds L., 231.
Zimmermann, Bruno, 768.
Zykmundová, Anna, 363.

TITLE INDEX

ABC pol sci, 472
ABS guide to recent publications in the social and behavioral sciences, 602.
Administration of criminal justice, 118.
Administration of United States foreign affairs, 720.
Administrative reforms in Pakistan, 444.
Africa today, 4.
African governmental systems in static and changing conditions, 11.
American-Chinese relations, 722.
American diplomacy, 724.
American doctoral dissertations on the Arab world, 15.
American foreign relations, 725.
American independence, 749.
American judge, 249.
American pamphlet literature of public affairs, 491.
American political parties, 471.
American political science review, 474.
American politics and elections, 462.
American state government and administration, 670.
Americans and Chinese, 723.
Anglo-American law collections, 332.
Anglo-American legal bibliographies, 39.
Annotated bibliography of bibliographies of statutory materials of the United States, 340.
Annotated bibliography of management information systems, 378.
Annotated bibliography of SOLO publications, 395.
Annotated bibliography of selected unclassified materials published during 1966 on problems of development and internal defense, 784.
Annotated bibliography on environmental perception, 72.
Annotated bibliography on Mississippi's economy, 404.
Annotated bibliography on Pennsylvania State Government, 455.

Annotated bibliography, urban and suburban politics, 389.
Annotated list of selected United States Government publications available to depository libraries, 734.
Annual legal bibliography, 273.
Anthropology in government, 527.
Aparthied, 10.
Applications des calculateurs aux sciences humaines, 615.
Asia today, 19.
Asian developments, 18.
Assignments to accompany the use of Legal bibliography and the use of law books, 333.
Atlantic Community, 428.
Ausgewählte und kommentierte Bibliographie des revolutionären Sozialismus, 91.
Aussenpolitische Memoiren, 173.
Auswahlbibliographie zur europäischen Integration, 157.
Automation and law, 219.

Background reading list on psychological operations, with special emphasis on Communist China, 539.
Bail in the United States, 28.
Baltimore metropolitan area urban affairs bibliography, 30.
Basic bibliography in public personnel administration, 559.
Basic library in public administration, 542.
Basic Russian publications, 582.
Basic source materials in political science, 476.
Basic techno-legal bibliography for law students and young lawyers, 218.
Bibliografia de las conferencias inter-americanas, 453.
Bibliografía jurídica del Ecuador, 297.
Bibliografía para el temario del Congreso Cultural de La Habana, 694.
Bibliografía sobre "El aumento de la población y su incidencia sobre la infancia, la adolescencia, la juventud y la familia americana," 621.
Bibliografie bibliografií děl V.I. Lenina a literatura o Leninovi, 362.
Bibliografie k dějinám ČSR a KSČ 1917-1938, 125.
Bibliografie van het christen- en religieus-socialisme in Nederland, 657.

Bibliografie voor het overheidsbeheer, 549.
Bibliografija odabranih elanaka iz međunarodnog javnog prava objavljenih u domaćim i inostranim periodičnim publikacijama u periodu od 1955-1965, 229.
Bibliografisk introduktion til fremmed og komparativ ret, 285.
Bibliographia politica, 512.
Bibliographia sociologica, 607.
Bibliographic index, 34.
Bibliographical guide to Belorussia, 776.
Bibliographical guide to the law of the United Kingdom, the Channel Islands and the Isle of Man, 309.
Bibliographical introduction to nationalism, 418.
Bibliographical sketch of the laws of Massachusetts colony from 1630 to 1686, 385.
Bibliographie critique des ouvrages française relatifs aux États-Unis (1770-1800), 717.
Bibliographie d'Aristote, 16.
Bibliographie de l'administration publique, 550, 551.
Bibliographie de l'anarchie, 14.
Bibliographie der social-politik, 642.
Bibliographie des deutschsprachigen Schrifttums zum Ostrecht, 300.
Bibliographie des oeuvres de Karl Marx, 382.
Bibliographie des Socialismus und Communismus, 656.
Bibliographie des traductions des codes de droit privé des états membres du Conseil de l'Europe et da la Conférence de La Haye de droit international privé, 77.
Bibliographie des travaux français de médecine légale, 387.
Bibliographie: deutscher Militärverlag, 396.
Bibliographie du droit international, 240.
Bibliographie européenne, 160.
Bibliographie général des sciences juridiques, politiques, économiques et sociales, 302.
Bibliographie raisonnée du droit civil, 301.
Bibliographie sélective des livres, articles, et documentations traitant le sujet des problèmes administratifs africains, 540.
Bibliographie sélective d'ouvrages de langue française traitant des problèmes gouvernementaux et administratifs, notamment en Afrique, 541.

Bibliographie sélective sur l'organisation internationale, 222.
Bibliographie van regionale onderzoekingen op sociaalwetenschappelijk terrein, 632.
Bibliographie wirtschafts- und sozialwissenschaftlicher Bibliographien, 42.
Bibliographie zur europäischen Rechtsprechung betreffend die Entscheidung zu den Verträgen über die Gründung der Europäischen Gemeinschaften, 114.
Bibliographie zur Friedensforschung, 449.
Bibliographies, catalogues, checklists and indexes of Canadian provincial government publications, 52.
Bibliographies de l'OECE, 158.
Bibliographies on international relations and world affairs, 37.
Bibliography and legal history, 286.
Bibliography for gaming in urban research, 69.
Bibliography for the Honour School of Philosophy, Politics and Economics, 477.
Bibliography in politics, 478.
Bibliography, 1915-1957, Quincy Wright, 224.
Bibliography of abridgments, digests, dictionaries and indexes of English law to the year 1800, 305.
Bibliography of African bibliographies, 35.
Bibliography of African government, 7.
Bibliography of African law, 291.
Bibliography of bibliographies in political science, 493.
Bibliography of bibliographies of legal material, 277.
Bibliography of books on war, pacifism, nonviolence, 441.
Bibliography of British municipal history, 409.
Bibliography of civil service and personnel administration, 79.
Bibliography of crime and criminal justice, 119, 120.
Bibliography of early English law books, 304.
Bibliography of Edmund Burke, 48.
Bibliography of English constitutional history, 185.
Bibliography of English-language source materials on Thailand, 681.
Bibliography of Federal grants-in-aid to State and local governments, 184.
Bibliography of Indian law, 311.
Bibliography of international development, 691.

Bibliography of international law and continental law, 40.
Bibliography of Italian colonisation in Africa, 245.
Bibliography of jurisprudence, 251.
Bibliography of Latin America, 262.
Bibliography of Latin American bibliographies, 38.
Bibliography of municipal problems and city conditions, 407.
Bibliography of new guides and aides to public documents use, 183.
Bibliography of Oliver Wendell Holmes, 205.
Bibliography of peace research, 450.
Bibliography of political science, 475.
Bibliography of political theory, 498.
Bibliography of public administration, 547, 548.
Bibliography of public administration in Australia, 27.
Bibliography of published reports on TCR/ORA-sponsored research, 599.
Bibliography of selected materials relating to the legislation of the New Deal, 334.
Bibliography of social studies, 603.
Bibliography of South and Southwest China, 58.
Bibliography of South Dakota State Legislative Research Council publications, 663, 664.
Bibliography of Supreme Court Justices to 1963, 250.
Bibliography of the California Legislature, 49.
Bibliography of the constitutions and law of the American Indians, 214.
Bibliography of the Faculty of political science of Columbia University, 489.
Bibliography of the Hungarian revolution, 1956, 210.
Bibliography of the Monroe doctrine, 1919-1929, 406.
Bibliography of the published writings of John Stuart Mill, 400.
Bibliography of the studies on law and politics, 315.
Bibliography of the writings of Roscoe Pound, 533.
Bibliography of the writings of Roscoe Pound, 1940-1960, 532.
Bibliography of United States-Latin American relations since 1810, 727.
Bibliography on administration in East Africa, 8.
Bibliography on European integration, 155.
Bibliography on foreign and comparative law, 107, 270.

Bibliography on housing, building, and planning, for use of overseas missions of the United States Agency for International Development, 208.
Bibliography on Kenya, 253.
Bibliography on municipal government in the United States, 412.
Bibliography on political anthropology, 503.
Bibliography on public administration, 561.
Bibliography on public administration in Latin America, 667.
Bibliography on public enterprises in India, 180.
Bibliography on regional government, 369.
Bibliography on state and local government, 669.
Bibliography on systems, 437.
Bibliography on taxation in underdeveloped countries, 678.
Bibliography on Texas government, 680.
Bibliography on the Communist problem in the United States, 99.
Bibliography on the foreign relations of the Republic of Turkey, 687.
Bibliography on the International Court, 193.
Bibliography on the political and administrative history of Vietnam, 769.
Bibliography on the problem of change of scale in the social sciences, 622.
Bibliography on the urban crisis, 581, 762.
Bibliography on Western politics, 751.
Biblioteca istorica della autica e nuova Italia, 410.
Bibliotheca Indosinica, 21.
Bibliotheca realis iuridica, 281.
Bibliotheca Sinica, 53.
Biographical and historical index of American Indians, 215.
Blueprint for bibliography, 608.
Boeken over oorlog en vrede, 772.
Bøger og tidsskrifter i det administrative bibliotek, 546.
Books on communism, 92.
Both sides of 100 questions briefly debated, 516.
Brazil, 43.
Brief guide to the use of the government documents of Great Britain and the United States, 187.

Brief list of books on political parties before 1865, 465.
British government publications, 186.
British official publications, 191.
British public administration, 192.
Bronnen voor literatuuronderzoek, 610.
Buddhist political thought, 492.
Bulgaria, 47.
Bulletin of Far Eastern bibliography, 133.
Bulletin of the British library of political and economic sciences, 483.
Bürgerliche Theorien über unterent-wickelte Länder, 690.

Calendar of the correspondence of George Washington... with the Continental Congress, 750.
California politics and problems, 50, 51.
Canada français et l'Amérique latine, 261.
Canadian-American relations, 730.
Canadian political parties, 458.
Catalog cards in book form for United States Joint Publications Research Service translations, 624.
Catalog of African government documents and African area index, 6.
Catalog of international law and relations, 226.
Catalog of the Foreign Relations Library, 779.
Catalog of the public documents of Congress, 742.
Catalogue des périodiques à la Bibliothèque centrale du Ministère des Finances, 648.
Catalogue of books in all the libraries on the theory and practice of politics, 505.
Catalogue of reference documents, 188.
Catalogue of the books of the Manchester Incorporated Law Library Society, 307.
Catalogue of the law collection at New York University, 282.
Catalogue of the library of Sir Edward Coke, 271.
Catalogue of the library of the Law school of Harvard University, 274.
Catalogue of the manuscripts of Jeremy Bentham in the Library of University College, London, 31.
Catalogue of the Rajasthan High Court Library, 288.
Catalogue systematique de la Bibliothèque de la Chambre des représentants, 292.

Changes in Congress, 713.
Checklist & index of Congressional hearings, 360, 712.
Checklist of American Bar Association general publications, 329.
Checklist of books and pamphlets in the social sciences, 635.
Checklist of Economic Commission for Asia and the Far East documents, 707.
Checklist of legal periodicals available in the Law library, University of the Philippines, 287.
Checklist of legislative journals issued since 1937 by the states of the United States of America, 358, 359.
Checklist of paper-back books and reprints in political science, 499.
Checklist of publications of the sections and House of Delegates of the American Bar Association, 13.
Checklist of the special and standing committees of the American Bar Association, 12.
Checklist of United States public documents, 1789-1909, 743.
Checklist publications of the State of Ohio, 436.
Checklists of basic American legal publications, 346.
China, 64.
China, a critical bibliography 56.
China, 1957-July 1960, 57.
Chinese bureaucracy and government administration, 66.
Chinese law, 294.
Citizen and business participation in urban affairs, 765.
Civil defence, 76.
Civil rights and liberties in the United States, 78.
Code making in early Oregon, 317.
Codes and code makers of Washington, 348.
Colombia, 84.
Commercial law, 89.
Communism in Latin America, 98.
Communism in the United States, 101.
Communist China, 65.
Communist Eastern Europe, 149.
Community, 761.

Community development in urban areas, 103.
Comparative public administration, 554.
Comparative survey analysis, 569.
Complément à la bibliographie rwandaise, 589.
Comprehensive urban planning, 68.
Computer in the public service, 558.
Confession issue from McNabb to Miranda, 123.
Constitutional revision in the Empire State, 110.
Contemporary social theory, 605.
Contribution towards a bibliography dealing with crime and cognate subjects, 115.
Contributo alla bibliografia del liberalismo nel mondo, 364.
Council-manager government, 413.
Cumulative bibliography of Asian studies, 440.
Cumulative index of congressional committee hearings, 361.
Current bibliography and abridged directory of the American right-wing, 756.
Current bibliography on Ethiopian affairs, 146.
Current checklists of State publications, 736.
Current issues, 706.
Current political science publications in five Chicago libraries, 490.
Current research in international affairs, 238.
Current research on the Middle East, 422.
Current research projects in public administration, 544.

Deans' list of recommended reading for prelaw and law students, 342.
Debate on the legal regime for the exploration and exploitation of ocean resources, 380.
Decision-making, 126.
Department of State publications on diplomatic history, international law, and the conduct of foreign relations, 714.
Desarrollo de la comunidad, 102.
Deutsch-französischen Beziehungen im Spiegel der DDR-Literatur, 172.
Deutsche Dissertationen zur Zeitgeschichte, 32.
Developing nations, 697.
Development and impact of British administration in India, 213.

Developmental change, 563.
Directories of Government agencies, 716.
Directory of planning, budgeting and control information, 555.
Disarmament, 129.
Dizionario bibliografico di opere giuridiche, 284.
Documentos oficiales de la Organización de los Estados Americanos, 439.
Documents of international organizations, 234.
Documents of New Jersey local governments, 373.
Drug addiction, 415.

E.E.C. and developing nations, 154.
East Asia, 135.
East Asia: checklist of literature proposed for micropublishing, 134.
East Central Europe, 147.
East Europe, 148.
Electoral college, 534.
Elementi per una bibliografia sui temi dello sviluppo economico, sociale e territoriale con particolare riguardo all'Emilia Romagna, 577.
Emerging nationalism in Portuguese Africa, 419.
Entwicklungsländer-Studien, 692.
Environmental planning, 145.
Environmental reform in the United States, 71.
Equal employment opportunity, 130.
Essai de bibliographie des principaux ouvrages de droit public, 1.
Étude des bibliographies courantes des publications officielles nationales, 36.
European and Atlantic affairs, 778.
European Economic Community, 151.
European international organizations and integration movements, 159.
Evidence and bibliography, 220.
Executive leadership in the public service, 565.
Exhibit and bibliography of current and supplementary materials on social, economic, and political problems, 618.

Fachgruppenkatalog: Gesellschaftswissenschaften, 626.
Far East, 132.
Federalism, 161.

Federalism and intergovernmental relations in Australia, Canada, the United States and other countries, 162.
Felix Frankfurter, 168.
Fifty years of Chinese communism, 96.
Filosofia del dritto e dello stato, 323.
Financing State and local government in Oregon, 367.
Finding list of the social sciences, political science, law, and education, 518.
Foreign affairs bibliography, 239.
Foreign area and foreign policy research papers, 728.
Foreign Office confidential papers relating to China and her neighbouring countries, 62.
Fortegenelse over dansk materiale til studiet af skandinavisk forsvars-og alliancepolitik, 1848-1950, 127.
Free and inexpensive materials on world affairs, 782.
Free speech bibliography, 365.
Freedom Institute bibliography, 682.
Freedom of the press, 366.
French Fifth Republic, 166.
French political pamphlets, 1547-1648, 167.
From now on ... an environmental bibliography, 144.
From radical left to extreme right, 758.
Fundamentals of public international law, 228.

Gallringslista och förteckning över aktuell juridisk literatur, 327.
Game theory and its application to the social sciences, 169.
General bibliography on international organization and post-war reconstruction, 232.
Geography of elections, 140.
German foreign policy, 1890-1914, and colonial policy to 1914, 171.
Geschichte und Literatur der Staatswissenschaften in Monographien dargestellt, 511.
Ghana, 179.
Government administration in South Asia, 662.
Government: classification schedule, classified listing by call number, author and title listing, chronological listing, 521.
Government document bibliography in the United States and elsewhere, 732.
Government of metropolitan areas, 408.

Government publications catalogue, 190.
Government reference books, 733.
Guide to bibliographic tools for research in foreign affairs, 242.
Guide to Commonwealth law reports, legislation and journals in the Lincoln's Inn Library, 280.
Guide to Federal career literature, 80.
Guide to foreign legal materials: French, German, Swiss, 303.
Guide to foreign legal materials: Italian, 314.
Guide to Japanese reference and research materials in the field of Political Science, 247.
Guide to law reports and statutes, 308.
Guide to League of Nations publications, 352.
Guide to library resources for political science students at the University of North Carolina, 485.
Guide to material on crime and criminal justice, 116.
Guide to published United States Government documents pertaining to Southeast Asia, 1893-1941, 23.
Guide to readings in civic education, 644.
Guide to reference materials in political science, 647.
Guide to research in United Nations law, 231.
Guide to research material in political science, 519.
Guide to selected United States Government publications, 746.
Guide to the diplomatic history of the United States, 1775-1921, 719.
Guide to the literature of social welfare, 651.
Guide to the study of international relations, 244.
Guide to the use of United Nations documents, 701.
Guide to U.S. Government serials & periodicals, 731.

Handbuch der Litteratur des Criminalrechts, 122.
Hawaii State research inventory, 202.
Hawaiian politics, 203.
Historical background of Pakistan, 212.
Historical statistics of Australia, 26.
Human relations in public administration, 545.
Hungarian Soviet Republic, 209.

Immunities in international law, 128.
Index of legal medicine, 388.
Index to legal periodical literature, 319.

Index to legal periodicals, 320, 321.
Index to legal theses and research projects, 328.
Index to multilateral treaties, 685.
Index to the publications of the United Nations, 704.
Indice militar colombiano, 397.
Indonesia, 216.
Information sources in the social sciences, 639.
Informations bibliographiques et documentaires en science politique, 780.
Intergovernmental relations in the United States, 163.
International administration, 237.
International bibliography of political science, 500.
International bibliography of public administration, 564.
International communication and political opinion, 567.
International communication and political warfare, 538.
International communications, 384.
International communist development, 93, 94.
International developments, 785.
International institutions and international organization, 223.
International law and organization, 230.
International organization, 236.
International political science abstracts, 501.
International politics, 781.
International socialist bibliography, 655.
Internationale communiste et les problèmes coloniaux, 86.
Internationalen Wirtschaftsorganisationen im Schrifttum, 235.
Inter-university research program in institution building, 479.
Introdução aos estudos históricos e sociais, 606.
Introduction to materials for ethnic studies in the University of Southern California Library, 401.
Inventories of Tennessee county records on microfilm, 113.
Inventory of research resources concerning a state-wide planning program for Minnesota, 576.
Israel legal bibliography in European languages, 312, 313.
Ius Americanum, 344.

Japan and Korea, 248.

Japan-Bibliographie, 246.
Japanese-sponsored governments in China, 1937-1945, 59.
Japanese studies of modern China, 54.

K stému výročí narození V.I. Lenina, 363.
Karl Marx, 381.
Kennedy literature, 252.
Key to League of Nations documents, 354.
Kolumbien, 85.
Kommunens styre og forvaltning, 371.
Kommunismus in Geschichte und Gegenwart, 95.
Korean views of America, 721.
Korean war, 255.
Krieg in Vietnam, 771.

Latin America, 666.
Latin America and the Caribbean, 265.
Latin America today, 258.
Latin American political parties, 460, 461.
Latin American studies in the non-Western World and Eastern Europe, 263.
Latin American urbanization, 67.
Latvia, 268.
Law books for non-law libraries and laymen, 343.
Law books in print, 338, 339.
Law books recommended for libraries, 269.
Law corporations, 355.
Law enforcement training materials directory, 350.
Law in the United States of America, 331.
Leaders of twentieth-century China, 61.
Learned Hand, 201.
Legal bibliography, 272.
Legal bibliography and legal research, 345.
Legal bibliography and the use of law books, 335.
Legal bibliography of the British Commonwealth of Nations, 306.
Legal periodicals in the United States Department of the Interior Library, 347.
Legal sources and bibliography of Bulgaria, 293.
Legal sources and bibliography of Czechoslovakia, 296.
Legal sources and bibliography of Hungary, 310.
Legal sources and bibliography of Poland, 324.

Legal sources and bibliography of the Baltic States, 298.
Legal sources and bibliography of Yugoslavia, 349.
Legislative process, 357.
Library of the Peace palace, documentation centre, 452.
Library resources for political science in Milwaukee, 520.
Life, liberty, and law, 515.
List of books in sociology and political science, 502.
List of books on social reform, 609.
List of books on West Indian federation, 775.
List of cabinet papers, 189.
List of Colonial Office confidential print to 1916, 195.
List of Colonial Office records, 196.
List of Foreign Office records, 197, 198.
List of official publications not included in the general catalogue of Government of India publications, 211.
List of publications issued by Committee on Banking and Currency, 738.
List of publications issued by the Dept. of Information, Republic of Indonesia, 217.
List of references on party government, 466.
List of references on the national committees of political parties, 467.
List of serials held in Law School Library, Sydney University, 289.
List of treaty collections, 686.
List of works relating to political parties in the United States, 468.
Literatur-Verzeichnis der politischen Wissenschaften, 628.
Literature of communism in America, 100.
Literature of political economy, 504.
Literature of political science, 486.
Literature of the rebellion, 748.
Literature of the social sciences, 627.
Literature on parole, 446, 447.
Local government in New York State during the Dutch period, 374.
Local government in West Africa, 370.
London bibliography of the social sciences, 629.
Luettelo, 165.

Man and environment, 108.
Man and his environment, 528.
Management, 543.
Managing overseas personnel, 715.
Manual of answers to accompany Legal bibliography and the use of law books, 336.
Mao papers, anthology and bibliography, 379.
Marx Károly Közgazdaságtudományi Egyetem oktatóinak szakirodalmi munkássága, 1945-1968, 611.
Materials and methods of legal research, 276.
Materials for the study of Federal Government, 759.
Materials for the study of politics and government in the Dominican Republic, 131.
Materials on legal bibliography, 283.
Metropolis, 368.
Metropolitan communities, 411.
Mexico, 390.
México en el siglo xx, 391.
Michigan State and local government and politics, 394.
Militärwissenschaftliche Quellenkunde, 398.
Minority groups, 403.
Missouri State government documents, 405.
Modern world, a political study syllabus, 786.
Monthly catalog of United States Government Publications, 744.
Monthly checklist of State publications, 739.
Mouvements ouvrier et socialiste, chronologe et bibliographie, 652.

NACLA research methodology guide, 600.
NATO, 435.
NATO bibliography, 431.
NORC social research, 1941-1964, 650.
Nation building and economic modernization, 699.
National development, 1776-1966, 138, 595.
Nationalism and national development, 417.
Nationalipolitische Publizistik Deutschlands von 1866 bis 1871, 174.
Natural resources in the governmental process, 109.
Neighborhood conservation & property rehabilitation, 766.
Neue politische Literatur, 633.
Neuere Studien zur Politik Brasiliens, 44.

New Afro-Asian states in perspective, 2.
New communities, 75.
New England development bibliography, 573.
New Studies; a guide to recent publications in the social and behavioral sciences, 634.
Nigerian official publications, 426.
Nikolai I. Bukharin, 46.
Non-GPO imprints received in the Library of Congress, 740.
Non-violent action, 448.
North Korea, 254.
North Vietnam, 770.
Not just some of us; a limited bibliography on minority group relations, 402.
Nuclear weapons and NATO, 432.

Official defense publications, 747.
Official publications of French West Africa, 9.
Official publications of Somaliland, 660.
Økonomisk og politisk litteratur om udviklingslandene, 695.
Open literature publications of the Social Science Department, 613.
Organization & methods, 557.
Organizing for national security, 760.
Orientering i samhällsfrågor, 676.
Ortak Pazar bibliyoğrafyasí, 152.
Overseas Chinese, 60.

PAR index, 375.
Pakistan, 442.
Pamphlets on public affairs for use in social studies classes, 623.
Panorama of recent books, films, and journals on world federation, the United Nations and world peace, 243.
Pariser Friedenskonferenz 1919 und die Friedensverträge 1919-1920, 445.
Personnel policies and practices, 457.
Philosophy, 508.
Planowanie regionalne, 578.
Point four: Near East and Africa, 423.
Police-community relations, 570.
Police literature, 351.

Political behavior, 646.
Political dimensions of rural development in Latin America, 266.
Political economy and political science, 643.
Political economy of the Middle East, 421.
Political elites, 142.
Political parties in the United States, 1800-1914, 464.
Political science, 494.
Political science; a selected bibliography of books in print, 507.
Political science and international relations, 513.
Political science, government & public policy series, 517.
Political works of concealed authorship in the United States, 1789-1910, 754.
Political writings in the young Republic, 755.
Politics of the new states, 674.
Politische Ideen in der freien Welt, 506.
Popular names of U.S. Government reports, 741.
Position classification and pay in the Federal Government, 81.
Poverty in the United States during the sixties, 530.
Poverty, rural poverty and minority groups living in rural poverty, 529.
Poverty studies in the sixties, 531.
Preliminary bibliography on studies of the roles of military establishments in developing nations, 17.
Preparation of briefs, 45.
Presidential inaugurations, 536.
Presidential succession, 535.
Problems of the Pacific, 136.
Process of modernization, 594.
Program und Wirklichkeit, 221.
Progress of Nigerian public administration, 427.
Propaganda and promotional activities, 537.
Public administration bibliography, 456.
Public administration in Pakistan, 443.
Public employment bibliography, 143.
Publications of the European Communities, 153.
Publications of the Institute of Government, 433, 434.
Publications of the International Court of Justice, 194.
Publications of the New Jersey Dept. of Community Affairs, 424.

Publikace Spojených národů v Universitní knihovně v Brně, 702.

Quarterly check-list of economics & political science, 523.
Quellenindex zur Cubakrise, 726.

Radical periodicals in America, 1890-1950, 654.
Read your way to world understanding, 700.
Reader's guide in economic, social and political science, 480.
Readers' guide to Britain and the European communities, 156.
Readers' guide to the Commonwealth, 90.
Reader's guide to the social sciences, 620.
Reading guide in politics and government, 752.
Recent publications on governmental problems, 560.
Recent research on political socialization, 526.
Recognition in international law, 572.
Recommended non-legal reference books for law libraries, 279.
Records of the Foreign Office, 199.
Records of the Socialist Labor Party of America, 658.
Référence et bibliographie en sciences, 614.
Reference guide to the study of public opinion, 568.
Regional economic analysis in Britain and the Commonwealth, 575.
Regional planning publications in Connecticut, 574.
Register of legal documentation in the world, 278.
Répertoire des périodiques, 420.
Répertoire des publications des partis politiques français, 459.
Reprints: economic and allied social science classics, 604.
Research in transportation, 683.
Research inventory for Wisconsin, 777.
Research materials for Slavists, 735.
Research materials for the study of Latin America at the University of Texas, 264.
Research materials in the social sciences, 612.
Research resources; annotated guide to the social sciences, 630.
Researches in political-science in India, 524.

Resources for teaching about the United Nations, 705.
Revolution and elite access, 579.
Revolution and structural change in Latin America, 259.
Revolutionary Cuba, 124.
Richard Hooker, 206.
Riots and demonstrations, 580.
Role of political parties in Congress, 463.
Rural Turkey, 688.

Science politique en France, 510.
Science, technology, and American diplomacy, 592.
Science, technology, and public policy, 590.
Scientific policy, research and development in Canada, 591.
Scrittori politici italiani, 481.
Select bibliography: Asia, Africa, Eastern Europe, Latin America, 82.
Select bibliography of Soviet publications on Africa, 5.
Select bibliography on British aid to developing countries, 137.
Select bibliography on traditional and modern Africa, 3.
Selected and annotated bibliography on politics in New Mexico, 425.
Selected bibliography: Michigan government and politics, 393.
Selected bibliography of biographical sources for the state governors of Michigan, 392.
Selected bibliography of Colorado State and local government, 87.
Selected bibliography of legal and other materials relating to the National Industrial Recovery Act, 416.
Selected bibliography of Maryland State and local government, 383.
Selected bibliography of materials in State government and politics, 671.
Selected bibliography of paperback books on crime, 117.
Selected bibliography of recent works in English on political processes in Malaysia and Singapore, 377.
Selected bibliography on Georgia government, 170.
Selected bibliography on Latin American government and politics, 267.

Selected bibliography on legislative apportionment and districting, 139.
Selected bibliography on Massachusetts politics and government, 386.
Selected bibliography on the history of the United States Supreme court, 763.
Selected bibliography on trends in legal education, 326.
Selected guide to annotated sources in political science, 495.
Selected list of books and periodicals in the field of personnel administration and labor-management relations, 553.
Selected list of recent books on modern political systems, 106.
Selected list of references on the convention system, 469.
Selected United States Government publications, 737.
Selective bibliography on State constitutional revision, 111.
Selective subject index: PAR research, 376.
Selective survey of English language studies on Scandinavian law, 325.
Serial bibliographies in the humanities and social sciences, 41.
Serial publications in the British Parliamentary papers, 200.
Serial publications of the Government of Fiji, 164.
Short guide to the literature of the social sciences, 638.
Short list of references to recent writings on American politics and political parties, 470.
Simulation of organizations, 593.
Social change in Turkey since 1950, 689.
Social science abstracts, 640.
Social sciences and humanities index, 641.
Social sciences general references, 522.
Social stratification, 596.
Social studies, 601.
Social studies bibliography, 637.
Socialism and American life, 653.
Sociology of the law, 659.
Solutions to the assignments to accompany Legal bibliography and the use of law books, 337.

Source material for the study of public administration, 556.
Source materials in public administration, 562.
Sources and problems of bibliography in political science, 496.
Sources for the study of the administration of criminal justice, 121.
Sources of historical election data, 141.
Sources of information; a handbook on the publications of the League of Nations, 353.
Sources of information on social issues, 598.
South Asia, 661.
Southeast Asia, 25.
Southeastern Europe, 29.
Southern Asia, 22.
Soviet armed forces books in English, 586.
Soviet disarmament policy, 588.
Soviet military power, 587.
Soviet Union, 583.
Spinoza bibliography, 668.
State constitutions and constitutional revision, 112.
State government and administration, 673.
State manuals, blue books, and election results, 672.
States and the urban crisis, 74.
Storia delle dottrine politiche, 509.
Strikes by public employees and professional personnel, 675.
Student politics and higher education in the United States, 83.
Student's guide to materials in political science, 488.
Student's guide to United Nations documents and their use, 703.
Studies in social and political behavior and change: Communist China, 63.
Study guide for Ghana, 178.
Study of subject bibliography with special reference to the social sciences, 631.
Study of the Columbia university library's acquisitions in political science, 482.
Studying the world, 783.
Subject bibliography of the social sciences and humanities, 617.
Subject guide to publications of the International Labour Office, 597.

Suggested library in public administration, 552.
Suggestions for a basic economics library, 625.
Suggestions for a basic political science library, 497.
Supreme Court of the United States, 764.
Survey of bibliographies in Western languages concerning East and Southeast Asian studies, 20.
Survey research on comparative social change, 693.

Tables of and annotated index to the congressional series of United States public documents, 745.
Tanzania, 677.
Teknisk udvikling i u-lande, 698.
Television in government and politics, 679.
Tentative check list of social science periodicals and monograph series, 619.
Théorie générale des institutions politiques des pays en développement, 696.
Theses in the social sciences, 645.
Thomas Hobbes, 204.
Thomas Hooker, 207.
To end war, 454.
Történelem, forradalom, 97.
Transportation in American history, 684.
Treasures and trivia; doctoral dissertations on Southeast Asia accepted by universities in the United States, 24.
Tribes of Yemen, 790.
Two world wars, 773.

USSR: strategic survey, 585.
Unauthorized practice source book; a compilation of cases and commentary on unauthorized practice of the law, 330.
Union catalogue of Western social science periodicals, 649.
Union list of basic Latin American legal materials, 316.
Union list of Commonwealth and South African law, 295.
Union list of foreign legal periodicals of the Southwest Chapter of the American Association of Law Libraries, 322.
Union list of legal periodicals, 318.

Union list of selected western books on China in American libraries, 55.
Union list of United States legal literature, 341.
Union list of West European legal literature, 299.
United Nations and related organizations, 711.
United Nations documents index, 709.
United Nations publications, 710.
United States and Europe, 788.
United States and Western Europe, 729.
U. S. treaties and agreements with countries in Africa, 718.
University research in government, 525, 566.
Unser Staat, unser Stolz, 176.
Urban affairs bibliography, 70.
Urban community development, 104.
Urban government manpower, 414.
Urbanization in West Africa, 767.
Useful translations of East European statutes in French and German, 150.

Veröffentlichungen über modern Politik und Geschichte der iberoamerikanischen Länder, 260.
Verzeichnis der in der Bibliothek des Bundesministeriums für Wirtschaft vorhandenen Gutachten, 616.
Vitae Germanorum jureconsultorum et Politicorum, 473.
Vom Pecht im Rheinland, 290.
Von der Wartburg bis nach Usedom, 175.

Water law bibliography, 774.
White collar crime, 88.
World affairs, 787.
World bibliography of bibliographies, 33.
World of cities, 73.
World organization, 233.
Worldwide bibliography of space law and related matters, 665.

Zusammenstellung der von der "Deutschen Demokratischen Republik" seit deren Gründung (7. Oktober 1949) abgeschlossenen internationalen Verträge und Vereinbarungen, 177.

Ref
Z
7161
A1
H35
v.1